The Missing Peace

Recovering a Whole Life
In a Broken World

STEVE EVANS

Healing
Streams
forerunner
PUBLISHING
Savannah, Georgia

The Missing Peace: Recovering a Whole Life in a Broken World
2012 by Steve Evans
Abridged from *Matters of the Heart: A Workbook for Personal Transformation*
Copyright © 2011 by Steve Evans

Distributed by Healing Streams Ministry, a division of Forerunner Ministries, Inc.
4625 Sussex Place, Savannah, GA 31405
Email: info@healingstreamsusa.org
Website: www.healingstreamsusa.org

Published by Forerunner Ministries, Inc.
ISBN-13:978-0615597928
ISBN-10:0615597920

Edited by Anne-Marie Evans.

Unless otherwise indicated, all Scripture quotations are from The Holy Bible, English Standard Version® (ESV®), copyright © 2001 by Crossway, a publishing ministry of Good News Publishers. Used by permission. All rights reserved.

Scripture quotations taken from the Amplified® Bible, Copyright © 1954, 1958, 1962, 1964, 1965, 1987 by The Lockman Foundation. Used by permission. (www.Lockman.org)

Scripture quotations marked (WEB) are from The World English Bible (public domain).

Scripture quotations marked (KJV) are from The Holy Bible, King James Version (public domain).

Cover and interior design by Forerunner Publishing, Savannah, Georgia. Cover image used with permission from Microsoft.

Printed in the United States of America by CreateSpace.

TABLE OF CONTENTS

The Journey Forward

The Way of the Cross

Healing Streams Ministry
The eCourse for Healing
Spirit Filled Living
Books from Forerunners

PREFACE

If you have had a taste of the marvelous peace of Christ and want to learn how to live consistently in it then this book is for you. A heavenly peace—gentle and uplifting, resplendent with hope and pregnant with possibilities for joy—is your true inheritance in Christ. Whether you are a brand new Christian or a veteran of many campaigns, this peace is meant to be your daily, moment by moment, experience of your union with Him, even and especially, in the midst of all the cares and pressures of this life. Sadly, this peace is *the missing piece* in many Christians' experience of their faith. We have Bible studies, church services, prayer and fellowship enough to fill our days, but this peace was meant to fill our hearts.

How can it be that the peace of Christ has gone missing? Is this not the peace of which Jesus said, "Peace I leave with you, My peace I give to you; not as the world gives do I give to you."?[1] The world is famous for its take backs. Jesus, on the other hand, makes His peace *always available* to us. Peace is His perpetual gift to us, but we are not living in it: What's going on?

Consider how the world gives beauty and strength to youth for free; riches, prestige and power to those who care for nothing else. It even gives a measure of peace to anyone on top of their game—whether it is self-protection or self-promotion—so long as you can see how things are going to work out in your favor. These gifts are all too often fleeting treasures. Yet, this peace that Jesus gives is intended to be an everlasting inheritance, *our* inheritance, our *daily* inheritance.

To be sure, most Christians can enter into this peace during an anointed worship service and can touch base with this peace during moments of devoted Bible study or prayer. We even have a rock bottom sense of peace that we are headed toward heaven and that God is in control. But do we *live in this peace* as our daily delight and source of surpassing strength—no matter what comes our way? That seems to be beyond us.

Throughout the Body of Christ there are those who suffer not only from diseases of the body but from the many and varied diseases of the soul: stressed by anxious concerns, carrying deep pain from the past, depressed in heart and spirit or just plagued by a whole host of negative emotions which can so easily quench the simple joy of living. Rather than being released into the glorious liberty of the children of God, many believers have become captive to their inner lives at the very time when the world needs a witness of the life-changing power of the gospel. As in Isaiah's day we are a people in need of restoration.

> **But this is a people plundered and looted; they are all of them trapped in holes and hidden in prisons; they have become plunder with none to rescue, spoil with none to say, "Restore!"** Isaiah 42:22

This book grew out of a conviction that there is a real power of transformation available through faith in Christ, but that His Words of life are somehow not reaching His people in a way that they can appropriate. As a pastor I knew the frustration of preaching and pleading, "Trust the Lord and follow Him," as the great answer to life's problems and a very real means of recovering peace, yet I rarely saw the needed changes come to others. I was gently haunted by a passage in Jeremiah about speaking words that do not heal.

> **They have healed the wound of my people lightly, saying, 'Peace, peace,' when there is no peace.** Jeremiah 6:14

I realized that others needed more, because I myself needed more. From the first moments of my new life in Christ, I had been introduced to the ministry of deliverance and have been gratefully walking in the benefits of that early release from demonic bondage ever since. But there would prove to be much more in the tangled mess of my innermost emotional life than could be addressed by simple deliverance. It was of course absolutely necessary—if I wanted freedom—to resolutely "put to death" anything that the Word or the Spirit identified as sin, lest I become enslaved to the enemy all over again. It was also essential that I learned to try my level best to trust the Lord and seek to follow Him—these two requirements of basic discipleship (along with Bible study, prayer, worship, fellowship and service) certainly bring tremendous comfort, growth and healing to those who walk in them. Basic discipleship helped me live with my pain and damaged inner life, it even helped me prune away the unwanted fruit, but it was not mending my heart or getting to the root issues that were causing me such abiding anguish.

Again and again I happily discovered that God was sending into my life two other graces that produced remarkable "results": strong revelation of truth and inner healing by His Spirit. Revelation and inner healing are therefore two goals of this series of lessons. Only the Holy Spirit can reveal truth in the way we need to receive it for its freedom-making power to liberate us; only the Spirit can do the transforming works of ministry necessary to restore our lost wholeness. However, there is much that we can do to position ourselves for grace to happen. Why else would He entreat us so often to seek Him?

These 24 lessons from Healing Streams Ministry's *Matters of the Heart* teaching series will show you how to bring your heart to God and how you can receive His Heart for you. That is the essence of the Great Exchange—our *dis*-grace for His grace—and it is always available for us to access through the faith He has given us. Where our inner state is concerned, there are two great assignments which are actually gracious invitations to experience the surpassing vitality of *new life* in Christ:

1) Restoration: Preparing our inward state to hold up under the pressures of daily life requires recovery of the natural grace that got lost along the way. For countless reasons—not least of which is getting free of the pain—we need to recover from any emotional brokenness emanating from our past. But there is another level…

2) Mastery: As we learn to manage our emotional life, we not only receive freedom from the past, but we gain the graced ability to reign with wisdom over our own emotions, making it possible to live even the most active or embattled days with deep peace and Spirit-led resourcefulness!

By a process of recovery leading to mastery we can experience our own life, no matter how damaged initially, becoming just what Jesus described to Nicodemus so long ago: weightless and free. Being "born again" is only the entry point. Those who learn this new way of yielding to His Spirit will become like leaves floating on the wind:

> **Do not marvel that I said to you, 'You must be born again.' The wind blows where it wishes, and you hear its sound, but you do not know where it comes from or where it goes. So it is with everyone who is born of the Spirit."** John 3:7-8

We truly can learn how to be lifted and carried by the river of peace that God is sending our way each day. Being born again ushers us into the new life; the Holy Spirit within us provides the power to live the new life. He is the River of Peace. Are you only experiencing trickles and puddles of that peace? Take these lessons to heart, learn *the way of the heart* and the peace will soon become a slender stream. Persevere and it will grow into a mighty river leading you into great adventures in company with your Lord. One Day it will carry you all the way to God's throne in heaven.

I leave it to God and the devil to provide the pop quizzes, times of testing and final exams. The Lord never tempts us at any time, but He does provide opportunities for growth. In our times of trial and struggle God is "testing" to see if we are ready and willing to take a step upwards into greater faith and faithfulness (He already knows our true spiritual condition, but do we?). Meanwhile the enemy becomes active, tempting us to come into agreement with his distorted perspective, take on his demented attitudes and walk in his destructive ways. I pray that you will learn to recognize the difference, shun the enemy and hearken to the Lord. May this become your time of learning these essential lessons of the heart and growing greatly in grace!

ACKNOWLEDGEMENTS

It takes the light of Christ, streaming to us through the scriptures, to enlighten our darkness and lead us out into the blessed sunshine of God's new day. Enough cannot be said in praise of God's Word, for upon it hangs our whole hope of liberation and transformation. That it was our Lord's own hope for us, too, is shown by His prayer to the Father, "Sanctify them by Your truth. Your Word is truth."[1] Ultimately, every word of truth that reaches us is lovingly sent by the Father of Light, who is Himself the giver of every good gift. Yet, we cannot help but thank the ones through whom that life-giving Word comes our way.

I feel such a debt of respect and gratitude for Dr. Henry W. Wright of Be In Health®. More than anyone else that I know, Dr. Wright has boldly wedded the findings of medical science with Holy Scripture and then carried them to their logical conclusion, reaping practical applications for healing with astonishing specificity. As he has shown in his book, *A More Excellent Way*, these previously uncharted depths of the soul hold the answer to one of life's most intriguing questions: Where does disease come from? Any informed reader of this book will quickly note my dependence upon many of Dr. Wright's basic categories and insights learned during unforgettable seminar sessions at his ministry base in Thomaston, Georgia beginning in the fall of 2000.

This workbook therefore owes much of its structure to the model for ministry that I saw in Thomaston, though there are many others I have learned from along the way. François Fénelon, Bishop of Cambrais and defender of Jeanne Guyon, is at the head of my list. I wanted out of my pain so badly! It took all the considerable kindness of Fénelon to persuade me that there can be no healing of anyone's life without an entire embrace of the cross. Let all who would be truly whole drink from the fountain of his wisdom and thank God with me that people in his day wrote such extensive letters! The Bibliography for further reading at the back of this book gives a more complete list of my indebtedness.

This book itself would never have come into being were it not for the polite entreaty of my wife Eunice, who championed the idea of a workbook from the beginning (of which this series of lessons is an abridgement) and who encouraged me to devote the time to its writing. At first all I could see was *more work*, but then as the vision developed and words seemed at times to leap upon the page, I became exhilarated with the hope that people all over the world would have access to the same truths and the very prayers that helped me bring my wounded heart to God and receive mending from His own Great Heart in return. May you find in Him, dear reader, all that He truly is!

SECTION ONE:
FOUNDATIONS

Keep your heart with all diligence,
For out of it is the wellspring of life.
Proverbs 4:23 WEB

CHAPTER 1

THE SPIRITUAL ROOTS OF DISEASE

Though we begin with the body, this series of lessons is not primarily about physical health and the means to achieve it. Rather, it is about seeking emotional and spiritual health of the highest order. Finding the life that is "hidden with Christ in God" or entering into "the glorious liberty of the children of God" would be excellent Biblical ways of expressing the goal.[1] As it happens, however, modern medical science shows us a connection between our emotional life and the root issues of disease that gives us a practical place to begin looking at our deeper, truer need. C. S. Lewis once described pain as "God's megaphone," meaning that He gets our attention when our bodies break down.[2] So, it is in seeking to find a remedy to our illnesses that we have been drawn into a far greater understanding of the ways in which we are actually going astray from our God. The diseases of our bodies are but reflections of the dis-ease of our souls!

Three Flawed Theories

Before we look at what is actually making us sick, let's go over some cherished notions that we may still be carrying around in the back of our minds. There are three flawed theories of why we get sick. They may not be taught, but they are often caught.

1) The germ theory: As an explanation of why we get sick, this is accurate but misleading, since germs account for only part of all diseases. Nor does this theory tell us why we had the weakened immune system that allowed germs to infect us in the first place. Stressing the body by lack of sleep, poor nutrition, or lack of exercise can weaken the immune system, but are you aware that research has shown that just six minutes of a negative emotion can suppress the immune system for more than 21 hours?[3]

2) The "out of the blue" theory: This provides a graceful covering for us, since we are claiming to have no idea of any connection between our lifestyle and the disease. (Surely it is

nothing we have done. It just came on us *out of the blue!*) Yet everything on earth happens by cause and effect. The real problem with this theory is that it seems to be pointing a finger at God who lives in those "blue" heavens. However, God is never the author of evil: Untainted by any shadow He is instead the Giver of "every good gift."[4] Death, disorders and disease are consequences of the fall of man.

3) The punishment theory: According to this theory we sinned, so God is punishing us. But that cannot be! God punished Jesus fully and completely at the cross for our sins; it would be a breach of justice for God to punish us when the penalty has already been paid in full by Another. A further problem is that it seems to suggest that God reaches, in anger, into His bag of punishments and puts one on us without regard to the natural order.

The Mind-Body Connection

The truth is that there is a natural connection between the way that we live and the diseases that come upon us. As much as 80% or more of all incurable diseases have a known mind-body connection. According to one study, stress related disorders account for 75-90% of all visits to primary care physicians.[5] Consider these connections between disease and emotional stress: high blood pressure and heart disease correlate with anger and hostility; autoimmune disorders, Multiple Sclerosis, Lupus and arthritis are associated with bitterness, resentments and self-hatred; gastrointestinal disorders such as IBS, panic attacks and heart palpitations are related to anxiety; tension and migraine headaches, along with back pain, TMJ and Fibromyalgia are all associated with repressed anger.[6] Now reflect that our science is just beginning to discover the linkages between specific negative emotions and specific physical disorders, but already these connections can be made. Imagine how fine-tuned this may one day become.

Negative emotions damage the body. When we perceive a situation to be dangerous, adrenaline and cortisol are released by our bodies to facilitate "flight or fight" responses. This is part of the

General Adaptation Syndrome (G.A.S.) which gives us the extra "gas" we need to power-up for potentially life-threatening situations. The problem is that most of the "dangers" that cause stress cannot be resolved by fighting or running away! Modern life seems to be characterized by a mounting sea of stressful events and daily pressures coming at people from every conceivable direction. And yet the real culprit isn't the situations which surround us—it is the emotional reactions going off inside of us. That is why Dr. Don Colbert entitled his book on the mind-body connection *Deadly Emotions*—not "deadly situations." Stating that emotions are not confined only to the mind or heart, he describes the physiological processes by which all emotions are translated into chemical reactions which occur at both the organ level *and* the cellular level! Apparently, the "most damaging" emotions are feelings we might consider "garden variety" such as un-forgiveness, anger, worry, fear and frustration.[7] Clearly, no one with an emotional life is immune to the danger!

These negative emotions which place so much stress upon our bodies come in two forms: those that arise out of present situations and those that are "embedded" in our deepest memories. Doctors Alexander Loyd and Ben Johnson in their book, *The Healing Code*, state that embedded negative emotions are the most damaging kind, producing "physiological stress" (at a subconscious level), as opposed to "situational stress" (at the conscious level).[8] These unhealed memories are actually stored as false beliefs and negative images which form "destructive cellular memories" in the cells of our bodies![9] In terms of the mind body connection they list three "one things" which we need to know: There is one thing that can heal anything—our immune system; there is one thing that turns off the immune system—stress; there is one thing that will turn the immune system back on—healing "the issues of the heart."[10]

From the Bible's perspective there are a few "good" emotions that we might perceive as negative ones due to the way that they feel: godly fear (awe and respect for God as both holy and all-powerful); "danger fear" (in life-threatening moments); righteous anger (hating the sin, yet still loving the person); and pure grief (mourning that is uncontaminated by anger, fear, doubt or guilt).

These emotions are actually very good to have even if they don't *feel* like it at the time.

From a medical point of view all other negative emotions are stressors to the body, and it is extremely evident how damaging they are to our physical health. However, from a Christian point of view they represent something that is also very damaging to our spiritual health—they are sins! Now this may seem like adding to the bad news: The negative emotions we don't like feeling in the first place are not only causing disease, they are also sins, separating us from God! Isn't this very bad news indeed? No, not at all: It is wonderful news! It shows us there is a way out, both from disease and from the entrapment of negative emotions.

If the negative emotions, causing us so much loss of peace and joy as well as health, are actually things in our personality that God has given us and wants us to have, then we are stuck with them—and the diseases they induce. However, if they are sins then He has provided a way of freedom, since Jesus died to free us from sin's power as well as from its penalty. That way of freedom will be the subject of all of the following lessons. For now let us consider the negative emotions in relationship to their polar opposite—the peace of Christ.

The Peace of Christ

We always have a choice how we will respond to life: Will we give in to stress, take on the negative emotions so close at hand, or will we choose to find the path of peace that comes from trusting and obeying God? God created us to live in peace with His peace. Even under the terms of the Hebrew covenant, it was possible to live with perfect peace, but there was a condition: Keeping one's mind fixed or stayed on the Lord. How does one do that? In a word—trust. Trusting God is how we "live by faith."[11]

You keep him in perfect peace whose mind is stayed on you, because he trusts in you. Isaiah 26:3

Peace comes to us on the basis of our actual heart-trust in God, not the doctrinal rightness of our beliefs. Our minds judge right and wrong, but it is with our hearts that we judge who to trust. Whenever we actually release our hearts to trust God, our minds naturally become rested or stayed upon Him, until something else disturbs our rest. In the New Covenant Jesus also promises us peace and His peace goes far beyond any of the outward things that disturb us.

> **Peace I leave with you; my peace I give to you. Not as the world gives do I give to you. Let not your hearts be troubled, neither let them be afraid.** John 14:27

How does the world give us peace? Anyone can get peace from the world in this way: *I see the problem; I go to work on it; I begin to see the thing get better; I get peace back.* You don't have to be a believer in anything but yourself to get peace in this way. But there are real problems with getting peace this way: *I can't always make things better so I lose even more peace in the attempt; I have to wait until things look like they are getting better before peace begins to return to me; and as soon as one trouble is fixed, I may lose peace over two more things that just flared up.* This way is guaranteed to produce many seasons of significant stress over the course of a lifetime. We know it all too well—it is the way of trusting Self to be our savior.

Jesus gives believing, trusting hearts peace at the first sign of trouble—whenever we cast our cares on Him as our only Savior.[12] All of us get a daily report card on how well we are doing at trusting and obeying the Lord. In fact it is personally delivered moment by moment as the Holy Spirit reveals our actual peace levels to us. In any moment the peace of Christ is either going up, holding steady, or going down—all according to our ability to trust and follow Jesus throughout the day.[13]

When our hearts and minds fully trust Him with the whole of our life and that of our loved ones, we are at peace. Our bodies can then experience peace (*homeostasis* or physiological equilibrium) and all systems work in balance to maintain health. As Dr. Art Mathias of Wellsprings Ministries in Alaska likes to say, our bodies are barometers of our spiritual health.[14] Seen in this light the diseases and disorders we can't ignore are "warning bells" alerting us of our need to return to living in the peace of Christ.

The Pathway of Disease

Pay close attention to this pathway of disease for it is also the way by which mental illness, addictions and all sinful behaviors become entrenched:

1) Loss of health comes from loss of peace in the mind or heart: This is the overwhelming evidence of mainstream science.

2) Loss of peace comes through the entry of negative emotions: This is simple displacement—after an internal "tug-of-war" either the peace of Christ or stress will always win out.

3) Negative emotions draw power from unresolved issues carried from the past: These are the root causes.

4) Unresolved issues always reveal that there are broken relationships of trust and love with God, self or others: The two Great Commandments have been breached.[15] These issues are crying out to be healed, not buried.

5) Loss of peace indicates there is a sin issue to deal with: We have been turning *from* God, which is why His peace was lifted.

6) Loss of peace warns that the other kingdom is manifesting through us: We have been turning *to* the enemy, which is why unchristlike thoughts and feelings are beginning to grip us.

Just as peace, love, joy and the other delectable fruit of the Spirit manifest the life of Christ and the working of God's Kingdom through us, so too do negative emotions actually manifest the "emotional life" of the enemy, coming out of our carnal or fallen nature, and advance his dark kingdom through us. We are paying a terrible price for not living in the peace of Christ.

Father, in the course of these lessons enable me to be honest, open and transparent before You. Please help me to choose to deal with You and with anything You may want to bring up. Despite the pain I may have to work through, I am determined to break free of my past and truly learn how to live with Your peace established in my heart.

CHAPTER 2

TRUTH OR CONSEQUENCES

We saw in the previous chapter that there is hope for becoming free of many illnesses, even addictions and mental disorders, since they are rooted in negative emotions and false beliefs that we can learn to overcome. However, this knowledge could become a heavy burden to bear for it means recognizing things we thought were "just emotions" as sins. Since we fall into these sinful emotional states so easily and so often, it begs the question: What is God the Father thinking and feeling about us? Is He angry? Is He losing patience? Is He withdrawing from us? Unless we can discover something about our Father God that will put our hearts to rest, this accurate view of sin could well become cause for even more stress! Thankfully, in God we have the perfect safety our hearts have been searching for all along!

Our homeword journey into His Heart of love begins by taking a necessary "detour" into the thorny question of suffering. Issues of disease raise questions about suffering, such as: Why does a good, *loving* God allow evil and suffering to exist? This series takes the following positions:

1) God is a thoroughly good God—unconditionally loving, abounding in mercy and yet completely just.

2) All suffering exists because evil exists—God is NOT the source or cause of evil.

3) All evil exists because of Satan's sin—his prideful free will decision to go a separate way from God. He led other created beings into rebellion with him, forming an empire of evil.

4) All suffering is due to three things: our free will *abused* (our sinful choices of thought, word or deed), a real world setting (which involves natural consequences for all choices) and the sins of an invisible enemy against us.

There has to be balance and an allowance for mystery when attempting to understand the relationship between God's sovereignty and human free will, as well as the painful issues of why a particular disease and suffering came about. Nevertheless the boundaries are clear: God is not the author of evil, Satan is. In heaven there is a complete absence of sin and suffering, because in heaven everyone is perfectly surrendered to God. We give the enemy countless open doors to bring sin and its consequences into our world through our lack of surrender, our sinful choices. God allows us to say "No!" to Him and to His ways. He does this for the sake of preserving our free wills. He even works through the evils our free will allows to restore us to love and to our lost humanity. Fortunately for us, He has many ways of turning our "No's" back into "Yes's," but in the interval much suffering can happen.

We don't seem to be as committed to our freedom of will as God is. We want *our* will to be free but not the will of others—especially if they are about to hurt us with it. Or we may want our wills to be free but don't want the real world consequences that go along with it. God, on the other hand, has placed all of us in a real world in which even the demons have freedom of choice. To live with a free will in a real world under assault by an invisible enemy, we will have to learn to love God's ways or face the consequences.

The Inescapable Reality

We have been given freedom of will and are therefore sovereigns over our own hearts. What we choose to believe in our mind and in our heart determines how we will react or respond to people and events.[1] Every emotion we have is springing up from the core of what we deeply believe. There is no neutral zone in this. We are either coming into agreement with God's truth in our thoughts, attitudes, words and actions, or we are moving into agreement with the enemy's lies.[2] Remember the peace report card from the previous lesson? Tragically, we have to make our decisions on faulty or incomplete understandings of truth and its consequences, all the while a cunning adversary is taking full advantage of our lack of knowledge to enslave us or destroy us.[3]

Truth or consequences is the unalterable rule of life. Since, our will does not operate in a vacuum, every thought we have—conscious or unconscious—has natural consequences in our bodies in terms of neurological or hormonal responses that affect our organs and even individual cells. That is the universe *within our bodies*. Our inner life also affects the universe *beyond our bodies* through our words, actions and prayers. We live in a very real world. Our choices truly matter. Even when we seem to have no power to make things better, we still hold great power to make them worse. This power is immense: We have actually been given the power to choose life or death.

> **I call heaven and earth to witness against you today, that I have set before you life and death, blessing and curse. <u>Therefore choose life</u>, that you and your offspring may live.** Deuteronomy 30:19

The Grace That Covers Us

Have you been dressed in stress? From the Bible's perspective, every negative emotion is a sin issue. When negative emotions turn our hearts away from trusting God and loving others, we are not clothed in Christ—which may be very often for some of us. How does the Father see us? Mercifully! Our Father covers us all with great grace. Grace is God's perpetual outpouring of love and mercy that we cannot earn and do not deserve. In revealing His glory to Moses, God could have shown him the starry heavens which declare His glory or He could have sent down the glory cloud that would one day fill the tabernacle and the temple.[4] But He didn't. Instead, He chose to reveal all that is magnificent about who He is. It is as if He said to Moses, "I'm glad you asked Me. So many of My children have such terribly wrong ideas about Me. Thank you for letting Me set the record straight and clear My own great Name."

> **Moses said, "Please show me your glory." And he said, "I will make all my goodness pass before you... The Lord passed before him and proclaimed, "The Lord, the Lord, a God merciful and gracious, slow to anger, and abounding in steadfast love and faithfulness, keeping steadfast love for thousands, forgiving iniquity and transgression and sin."** Exodus 33:18-19, 34:6-7

We are also shown the Father's glorious grace in the New Testament. The Father is fully reconciled to us. He has foreseen all that will be needed of suffering and sacrifice, of patience, mercy and grace *on His part* and He is "OK" with whatever is required to save us. In fact the Father was *in Jesus* reconciling the world to Himself. He did this by not holding our sins against us. Instead He held them against Jesus, so that we could receive newness of life.[5]

> **But all things are from God, who through Jesus Christ reconciled us to Himself** [received us into favor, brought us into harmony with Himself]... **It was God** [personally present] **in Christ, reconciling** *and* **restoring the world to favor with Himself, not counting up** *and* **holding against** [men] **their trespasses** [but cancelling them]**, and committing to us the message of reconciliation (of the restoration to favor).** 2 Corinthians 5:18-19 AMP

Apply this passage to negative emotions. God the Father is not "holding it against" us that we have so many negative emotions stressing us or depressing us. He is perfectly able to love us even when we are in the negative emotion "pig pen" feeding the swine! And He is continuously calling to us to come home to His loving embrace.[6] This is the truly Good News about His amazing grace.

God's Justice System

Then how does God correct the world? Will not the Judge of all the earth bring justice?[7] Yet He refuses to accuse or condemn us, He refuses to terrify or threaten us and He isn't counting our sins against us.[8] What is left? Love, truth and consequences. By His love, He draws all who are willing, and by His Word, He leads all who are willing (speaking through conscience, nature, scripture and others). If we are not turned into His ways by these "polite" methods, then He allows some of the consequences of our wrong choices to help us realize that we are heading in a wrong direction. Heart-peace, trust and mercy-giving love are the *only* way of life offered to us by God.

Even great grace such as we have been offered does not remove the necessity of our repentance. In the same passage in which He revealed His glorious grace to Moses, God also stated that He "by no means clears the guilty."[9] Since even grace cannot be forced upon anyone, there is only one way of removing sin and its consequences: repentance. Until we choose to change our ways, He "keeps" (stores up) mercy for us, but mercy cannot be released to do its full work of restoration until we repent and return to receive it.[10] When the children of Israel were about to enter into their Promised Land, the Lord told them to create a visual picture by having some men stand on Mt. Ebal calling down the curses that would come to those who would not listen and obey Him and others to stand on Mt. Gerizim calling down the blessings on those who would obey.[11] The choice is ours!

The Curse of the Law

Things that represent the "curse of the Law" (the consequence of sin) don't come to us accidentally.[12] The curse may enter our lives through three ways: the sins of others, un-repented sins of our forefathers (generational sins in the family or on the land), or our own sins of thought, word or deed whether known or unknown, including things done or left undone. It is a wonder any of us are sane and healthy! Actually, this too is due to His generosity for He doesn't treat us as our sins deserve.[13] Even so, sin's very real consequences always lead to death. No one gets away with any sin.[14] The law of sowing and reaping applies until repentance comes and even repentance doesn't remove all consequences, but it does allow God opportunity to bring restoration and redemption.[15] Consider the "little" sin of simple unforgiveness:

1) The first consequence of unforgiveness is that it immediately begins to rob you of joy.

2) Then you discover your peace slipping away whenever you think of what happened.

3) You discover the relationship being affected negatively.

4) The longer you hold on to it, the more the remembered pain of the event may intensify.

5) You become more critical not only of the person, but of other people in general.

6) As your walls go up you begin to feel cut off from God's Presence, His peace and joy.

7) As more walls go up, other relationships are affected.

8) More of your time is fruitlessly robbed from you by dwelling on the past.

9) Unforgiveness increases the stress load upon the body and can lead to illnesses.

10) And on and on…

Keys to Health and Freedom

Jesus gives us keys that provide access to His Kingdom's health and freedom. As we saw in Chapter 1, His summary of the Law clearly shows us that our primary assignment is to work at building (or rebuilding if need be) relationships of trust and love with God, self and others.[16] When these relationships are healthy, God can send many blessings our way—this is His desire. However, we "invite" the curse even in the form of disease when there is a breakdown in one or more of these relationships.[17] This means that there is tremendous hope for all of us that if we are willing to put our primary assignment *first* and do what is needed to get things right *in our hearts*, our bodies may very likely return to full health. Our hearts hold the key!

Keep your heart with all diligence, for out of it is the wellspring of life. Proverbs 4:23 WEB

Thank God, however, there is one dreaded consequence we never have to fear coming upon us: losing His love. He loves us *unconditionally*.[18] And that's the truth!

Father, there is so much I still don't understand, help me to walk in what I do know and come with further teachings so that I can grow. I cast this care on you. I suspect that there are so many things about me that need changing that I am overwhelmed. I cast the burden of my whole life on You. Thank You for taking on these cares and for having a plan already in place for helping me. I am ready to trust and obey You with whatever You show me is my part.

CHAPTER 3

THE KEYS TO THE KINGDOM

In the first two chapters we noted the powerful connection between our negative emotions and many diseases and the uncomfortable fact that such emotions of the carnal nature are actually sinful states. How are we to get free? As it happens Jesus has foreseen our need and promised us keys—keys to His Kingdom! In this chapter we will look at what the Kingdom of God means in terms of our daily experience, what the keys are and what it is that the keys unlock.

Jesus has given keys of access to His disciples. The keys are the power to bind and loose. We are to bind the enemy and carry his works captive to Christ and we are to loose people from their sins and release them to God, ourselves included. The keys enable us to access the powers of heaven.

I will give you the keys of the kingdom of heaven, and whatever you bind on earth shall be bound in heaven, and whatever you loose on earth shall be loosed in heaven." Matthew 16:19

What Is This Kingdom?

By the above text of scripture we see that these keys are meant to be used "on earth" and they are given to all who receive the same revelation that Peter received—the revelation of Jesus Christ, the Church's great foundation. This Kingdom is a present reality to all believers, but entering into it and accessing its power is evidently not automatic, which is why we need the keys.[1] Consider that every born again Christian receives the "starter kit": forgiveness of sins, the indwelling Spirit, hope of heaven, union with the Body of Christ, knowledge that the Bible is God's Word, and the revelation that Jesus is a very personal Savior and Lord. That's a lot! One would think that would be enough to set us forever free. Yet many experience defeated, miserable lives.

Perhaps, this explains why Jesus wants to give us keys. However, if we are to use the keys we will need to know what they are and what they are for. It will also help us to know some things about the Kingdom of God to which they give us access. A kingdom is the realm where a king reigns—the *king's domain*. Paul gives us a clear description of what the Lord's reign is like:

For the Kingdom of God is not eating and drinking, but righteousness, peace, and joy in the Holy Spirit. Romans 14:17 WEB

Righteousness in the sense of saving grace is "right standing with God"—given to us through the new birth and faith in what Jesus has done for us at the cross. Through justification God has forever separated us from our sins and given us a new righteous status *in Christ*, one we don't deserve because our actual "living" is not righteous in *all* our ways.[2] Yet this accurate definition of the righteousness that comes by faith may keep us from seeing the vast righteousness of the Kingdom because what is fully meant by righteousness includes everything that is right (good, beautiful and true) which flows from God: Lunch with a friend is righteous; doing a job well is righteous; playing with puppies and babies is righteous; enjoying a sunset or a good book is righteous. It certainly isn't unrighteous! In this wider sense righteousness is anything the Holy Spirit would lead you into doing or appreciating. Such righteousness is the very life of heaven on earth. This kind of righteousness by itself isn't sufficient to get anyone into heaven or the cross of Christ would not have been necessary, but this kind of righteous living is made possible to us through living *in the Spirit*. This is "Kingdom living" in very practical terms.

Like God's righteousness, the peace and joy of God's Kingdom are vast. His peace is different from the peace this world offers, which is so easily lost. The peace of His Kingdom is deep and everlasting—nothing on earth can shake it; nothing on earth can take it from you. Likewise, the world's pleasures are fleeting, but the joy of this Kingdom is available to everyone at any moment for it proceeds from the glad-hearted God who wants to share His joy with us. Unlike mere happiness which depends upon "things going our way," joy can come to us in any moment in which we realize by a living faith who we truly are in Christ and who our God really is. And who can say enough about the Holy Spirit? He is the very Presence and power of Jesus on earth today. This is what the Kingdom is "made" of! Now if we were suddenly told that all the right ways of living, all the peace, all the joy that we have ever wanted *and* the Presence and power of God were on the other side of town just waiting for us, we would be catching the next bus or taking off on foot.

Where Is This Kingdom?

Just where is this Kingdom to be found? Jesus told Nicodemus that unless he was converted (born again) he would neither be able to see this Kingdom nor enter into it.

> **Jesus answered him, "Most assuredly, I tell you, unless one is born anew, he can't see the Kingdom of God"... Jesus answered, "Most assuredly I tell you, unless one is born of water and spirit, he can't enter into the Kingdom of God!"** John 3:3, 5 WEB

Perhaps that has already happened for you. You can now "see" the Kingdom because you have eyes of faith to see the King. And you have been "translated" by the Father out of darkness into the Kingdom of His Beloved Son.[3] Conversion certainly gets us into a portion of the Kingdom, but are we still searching for entry to that place where all the righteousness, peace and joy can be found? Imagine how it would feel if you were conveyed to the airport of a foreign country, but never left the airport to explore the land or enjoy life with its citizens. So too we may be in the Kingdom of God, but still not be fully sharing in its life. And this life is all around us! Jesus tells us that it is literally as close as the air that we breathe—for it both surrounds and fills us. Amazingly, this Kingdom is always within reach of and always "hiding" inside every believer.[4] We are in it like fish in the sea: The fish is in the ocean and the ocean is in the fish. As Jesus said, we need to repent—change our way of thinking—and believe this good news!

The Master Key

Consider this: If all of these highly desirable things are already within us and are all around us, what is keeping us locked out? According to Jesus, conversion in the form of the new birth gets us into heaven; becoming as little children gets us into the Kingdom.[5]

It is a realm that apparently *requires* childlike trust and cleanness of spirit in order to enter it. In the following scripture note how stringent the warning is: Unless we "repent" (are converted) *and* become as little children we will *never* enter into His Kingdom. The "big key" is becoming like a little child!

> **And He called a little child to Himself and put him in the midst of them, and said, "Truly I say to you, unless you repent (change, turn about) and become like little children** [trusting, lowly, loving, forgiving]**, you can never enter the kingdom of heaven** [at all]**."** Matthew 18:2-3 AMP

Entering heaven is a pure gift of grace given to those who have saving faith in Jesus.[6] However, Jesus is not speaking about entry into heaven here. In Matthew's gospel the Kingdom of God on earth is usually referred to as the Kingdom of heaven. To this day little children enter the Kingdom on earth and show forth its fruit far better than most believers.[7] And this is true of little children no matter the religion of their parents. In fact most little children haven't even been converted (know and believe in the King) and yet they still live in His Kingdom. What is it about little children?

We can safely assume that Jesus wasn't holding up as an example a little child "in the flesh" but one that was in the right spirit. All such children exemplify the life of the Kingdom.[8] They are humble, unself-conscious, willingly dependent for all provision upon their parents and freely love the people they meet. They are also teachable, fearless explorers of their world and live with openness and transparency in the present moment. If anything troubles or hurts them they run to their parents, are quickly set right and easily let go. In fact when hurts begin to accumulate and they start carrying yesterday and its pains with them, children become self-protective, leave childhood behind and become *like us*—so *untrusting* that we now need faith in Christ to restore our lost access to God's Kingdom. Jesus says that self-protectiveness—trying to control our life and that of the ones we love—is guaranteed to rob us of life.[9] His Kingdom doors only open to trusting hearts! We need to take His warning to heart and seriously start learning how to "let go" so that we can reenter the life of grace and freedom we left behind.

Four Essential Keys

We lock ourselves up in a dungeon of pain and bondage without ever realizing what we are doing. Due to an accumulation of life's hurts that we did not release, we left childlikeness behind by binding the pains and injustices of the past to ourselves. Unforgiveness is the number one block to healing and to the Kingdom's peace and power. It leads to unanswered prayer, unreceived mercy, hardness of heart, spiritual bondage and painful inner torment.[10] Walls that were erected to keep us safe now imprison us and shut the Kingdom out.

And in wrath his master turned him over to the torturers (the jailers), till he should pay all that he owed. So also My heavenly Father will deal with every one of you if you do not freely forgive your brother from your heart *his offenses*. Matthew 18:34-35 AMP

Hidden and unrecognized unbelief can also bar our entry into the Kingdom because it "hardens" the heart before God as powerfully as un-forgiveness does. Unbelief kept the Israelites out of the land promised to them; it keeps us out of the life that has been promised to us.

Take care, brothers, lest there be in any of you an evil, unbelieving heart, leading you to fall away from the living God... So we see that they were unable to enter because of unbelief. Hebrews 3:12, 19

Without doubt there are many keys to the Kingdom: Some keys are for accessing the supernatural realm to gain power for miracles and healing; other keys are for advancing His governance over the spheres of power and influence that shape nations. Our focus, however, is upon establishing His Kingdom as a superior principle over our inner state, so that both recovery and mastery of the emotional life can be achieved. Towards that goal there are four keys that we will need to learn how to use—frequently!

Key #1) Receive: Confess and repent of recognized sin and receive full forgiveness (consider these as "halleluiah moments"—see below). Receive the grace offered to you.

Key #2) Release: Confess and repent of un-forgiveness and release full forgiveness (towards God, self or others—until no pain is left in the memories). Give grace freely to others.

Key #3) Believe: Confess, repent of unbelief and believe His truth with a full heart of faith.[11] No matter what, believe in God and His grace until you are fully liberated by believing truth.[12] This is our real work.[13]

Key #4) Discern: Use the key of knowledge: discerning the spirits; discerning truth.[14] This enables you to recognize which of the first three keys needs to be used.

Because God gives us sovereignty over our hearts, it is not what happened to us that is the real issue. It is how we have reacted to hurt and injustice that determines our life, our peace and our emotional freedom. Use the keys to forgive others and to fully accept yourself. At first it may seem like this teaching is making the problem worse because you are being shown the connection between physical, mental and emotional health and what the Bible clearly describes as sin issues: bitterness towards others, unbelief, envy, not accepting oneself, living full of stress, etc. However, through repentance, grace and faith there really is a pathway of cleansing and freedom. Learn to say "Halleluiah!" when the Holy Spirit reveals sin in you that you had not seen before—it means He is getting ready to cleanse you and give you greater entry. So, set your heart "on pilgrimage" and get really, really good at using these four keys.[15]

Father, thank You for translating me out of darkness and into the glorious Kingdom of Your Beloved Son! I repent of and renounce all false ideas about where the joy and peace are to be found. You have placed it all around me and within me! Thank You for giving me the keys to Your Kingdom. Help me to get really good at using them to unlock my heart from un-forgiveness towards myself and others and from all the ways in which I have not been believing in who You are and what You have promised. Thank You that it is Your desire to lead me into this Kingdom!

30

CHAPTER 4

KINGDOMS IN CONFLICT

In Chapter 3 we saw that Jesus has given us keys that give access to the peace and joy of His Kingdom on earth. These are divinely powerful keys guaranteed to work—but it is not so easy to get them to work. Someone is resisting us practically every step of the way! Satan's name actually means "Adversary"—the one who "opposes" and "plots against" God and us. In a strange way it is comforting to learn this truth that we didn't mess up our lives or the planet as a whole just by our own foolishness alone. We evidently had lots of help coming from an invisible realm that we may have had no idea even existed. There are plenty of people— including Christians—who don't believe the devil is real or that knowing about him could have any relevance for daily life. C. S. Lewis wryly commented upon this way of the world in his preface to *The Screwtape Letters*.

> There are two equal and opposite errors into which our race can fall about the devils. One is to disbelieve in their existence. The other is to believe, and to feel an excessive and unhealthy interest in them. They themselves are equally pleased by both errors.[1]

We certainly don't want to fall into the ditch of error on either side of this truth. The great thing in the Christian life is our relationship with Christ—not with the enemy. Even so this very deceptive enemy must be exposed in order to be successfully resisted. We would be wise to learn from the elders of the early church who tell us that they took care to beware.

To keep Satan from getting the advantage over us; for we are not ignorant of his wiles *and* **intentions.** 2 Corinthians 2:11 AMP

An Introduction to the Battlefield

Did you know that you have a personal enemy, even legions of enemies? Did you know that they know your weaknesses and will stop at nothing to bring you down? How can you survive on a battlefield, if you don't know that a war is going on? How can you

31

fight back, if you don't know who your enemy is, or how to recognize him or how to use your weapons? We have been given free will in a real world that is besieged by an invisible enemy.[2] None of us volunteered to be involved in this war—we were born into it. We can learn to fight in the great battle of our age, or be rendered ineffective, taken captive, or destroyed. We can even have a great love for God and still be defeated by a lack of knowledge.[3]

> **Therefore my people go into captivity for lack of knowledge.**
> Isaiah 5:13 WEB

> **My people are destroyed for lack of knowledge.** Hosea 4:6

This invisible kingdom of the enemy was in the Garden, but it was kept separate from Adam and, before the Fall, could not interfere with his fellowship with God. Tragically, after Adam and Eve sinned, the nature of Satan—his way of feeling, thinking and believing—began to operate in them and seemed like their own reasoning process.[4]

There are literally hundreds of references to evil spirits, fallen angels and Satan in the scriptures. Instances of demonic oppression abound. In the New Testament there is a linking of sickness and oppression, just as there is a linking of sickness and sin. There is not a shared identity of the two, but a relationship: Not every sickness required deliverance from demons: Not every deliverance from demons involved a physical illness. Nevertheless, disease and death come from the Fall, not the blessing of God. Hence, it is the enemy's kingdom that is at work behind sickness and disease to enforce the curse of the law.[5] Consider these examples:

> **They brought him all the sick, those afflicted with various diseases and pains, those oppressed by demons, epileptics, and paralytics, and he healed them.** Matthew 4:24

> **Behold, there was a woman who had a spirit of infirmity eighteen years, and she was bent over, and could in no way straighten herself up. When Jesus saw her, he called her, and said to her, "Woman, you are freed from your infirmity."** Luke 13:11-12 WEB

The spiritual realm of darkness is not inhabited by ethereal forces, but by intelligent beings with malignant natures. Evil spirits have personality, will and desire, but lack bodies through which to carry out their assignments. Jesus says evil spirits prefer to occupy our bodies and think of us as their "house."

> **"When the unclean spirit has gone out of a person, it passes through waterless places seeking rest, but finds none. Then it says, 'I will return to my house from which I came.' And when it comes, it finds the house empty, swept, and put in order. Then it goes and brings with it seven other spirits more evil than itself, and they enter and dwell there, and the last state of that person is worse than the first."**
> Matthew 12:43-45

The evil spirits that have been cast out and sent into "waterless places" are in torment because they need a means of expressing their nature. They need our agreements with them and the use of our bodies so that they can sin through us. Being in terror of their dark lord, they urgently desire to fulfill their mission by expressing themselves within us and to propel us by inward pressure (fear, anger, lust, shame, etc.) into outward sins as well. All the while they take an unholy pleasure in feeling inside of us the very feelings we don't enjoy; hence, their primary goal is to return to the person they were cast out of. We need to clean our "house" and keep it filled and guarded. Evil spirits gain dominion over us by tempting us to agree with the sin they represent (i.e. a "spirit of fear" promotes fear). Christians cannot be possessed by the enemy, since they are the Lord's possession.[6] However, they can be and often are oppressed from the inside and/or the outside by this infernal kingdom.

Discernment Is Key to Our Freedom

The enemy seeks to veil his work with darkness and deception—that's why discernment is one of the four keys to freedom (see Chapter 3). If we can recognize the working of this kingdom, we can overcome it for light drives out darkness.[7] If we do not discern the spirits, their position and power continues unchallenged. We enter into agreement with the evil spirit whenever we let it express itself through us. When that happens it is no longer sinning by itself—*against us*—its sin has become our sin—*within us*. Sin is an agreement with the enemy—with his ways, his perspective and his desires. Until we fully forsake a sin, we are still in "secret" (unrecognized) agreement with it at some level deep inside our heart. Because the evil spirits so thoroughly believe in the "rightness" of their demented perspective, we have to learn how to break our agreements with the compelling power of their entrenched beliefs.[8] We will have to work hard at believing God's truth instead. This is war and war is never easy, but our freedom is well worth the effort it takes.

Consider this in relation to the negative emotions. Every negative emotion has had its source in this kingdom all your life. These evil beings have been sinning against you from birth. We could all easily share David's complaint that an enemy has hated us and laid snares for us "without cause."[9] The kingdom of darkness is the true source behind all of your pain and suffering as well as your own sinful ways, but you didn't know this in the beginning. You looked around and all you could see was other people and the injustice coming through their sins against you. You were blinded from seeing these three things with enough understanding to stay free, but these truths can liberate you now:

1) The real enemy was the evil spirits who had attacked those people first and were using them against you.

2) In unintended reaction to your pain it was your own sinful reactions and ungodly beliefs that bound the pain to you.

3) The loving and faithful God was always there with you, preserving your life, just as He is with you now to heal your life.

Now, God is saying to you: *Forgive people for everything*—let Him deal with them—and concentrate on the real enemy. Confess your own sins (including any unforgiveness), resist Satan's kingdom and let God restore your life as you leave justice to Him. All the while, keep your focus on the Lord. Our primary objective is not to crush the enemy, but to love God with our whole being.[10] In terms of spiritual warfare, this translates into trusting and obeying God no matter what the enemy is doing—to surrender and stay surrendered to God. Consider this well: There is no peace without surrender. Yet, even believers often find themselves living without the peace of Christ capturing their hearts. The truth is that whenever we begin to move away from the place of total surrender, we are, *to that degree*, joining the Great Rebellion that began when the enemy used his free will to move away from the will of his Creator and go his own way. Since our ongoing surrender to the Lord is the key to victory, we will surely have to learn how to face the cross of our embattled times and say with Jesus, "Nevertheless, not my will, but Yours, be done."[11]

The Importance of a Fighting Spirit

The language of spiritual warfare can be found throughout the New Testament, but it is in the Hebrew Scriptures especially that we see the importance of maintaining a fighting spirit. The children of Israel could visibly see their enemy coming to steal, kill and destroy and they responded accordingly! Our battle is not against flesh and blood as theirs was for they were called to be examples to us (in the visible and natural realm) of things that we would experience in the invisible realm of our own spiritual warfare. We have to learn how to "see" by means of faith to win our battle.[12]

Now these things happened to them as an example, but they were written down for our instruction, on whom the end of the ages has come. 1 Corinthians 10:11

One of the things which caused the Israelites to stumble was a great fear about going up against the giants in the land that the Lord had promised to them as their inheritance. They were very reluctant warriors! However, in the battles to come, it was Joshua and Caleb who saw an opportunity for the people of God to grow stronger, just as fresh bread strengthens and revitalizes a hungry person. These men had faith that the God *they* believed in was capable of helping them gain the victories they needed against the giants, boldly saying the giants would be "bread for us."[13] Ultimately, it was *only* Joshua and Caleb of that generation who ended up enjoying life in the land promised to all of those who Moses led out of Egypt.

Whether you want it or not, one of the ultimate battles of life lies right before you—to subdue the interior landscape of your own heart by fighting to fully believe and do what God's Word declares to be truth.[14] What a conundrum it is that we have to be willing at times to fight to live in the Kingdom's peace and joy. Hebrews calls it laboring to enter the promised place of rest.

Let us labour therefore to enter into that rest, lest any man fall after the same example of unbelief. Hebrews 4:11 KJV

In the fourth and fifth centuries many noble souls "fled" the lukewarm Christianity of the converted Roman Empire to the deserts of Egypt in order to live more totally for Christ. They discovered that like Jesus they were to face some of the stiffest temptations from the enemy in their wilderness. They quickly discovered that it was easy to get the monk (the spiritual athlete, the God chaser) out of Rome, but far harder to get "Rome" out of the monk! Here are a few nuggets of wisdom gleaned by Henri Nouwen from the writings of the desert fathers:[15]

The chief task of the athlete is to enter into his heart [and do battle there]. - Macarius the Great, Desert Father, ca. 300-391.[16]

The great work of a man… [is] to expect temptations to his last breath. - Saint Anthony of Egypt, Desert Father, ca. 251-356.[17]

You should realize that as soon as you intend to live in peace, at once evil comes and weighs down your soul... But if we are vigilant, all these temptations fall away. - Mother Theodora, d. 490.[18]

Even so, the great thing is never the battle, but the "resting in the Lord" and the "flowing in the Spirit" times that lie on the other side of each fresh victory.

Father, thank You for the Blood of Jesus, the Name of Jesus, Your truth, Your Spirit and Your armor—my weapons for the "right hand and the left" for offense and defense.[19] You have truly equipped me for fighting the spiritual battles that lie ahead! I place the helmet of salvation over my mind and the righteousness of Christ over my heart. May I always be girded about by Your truth and may my feet remain upon Your path of peace. I take up faith as a shield against the Accuser and wield Your Word as a sword to cut through the darkness so that I can keep walking in Your light, praying always for Your Presence and power to guide me!

CHAPTER 5

SEPARATION FROM SIN

In the previous lesson we studied the rebel army and saw how its members work to bring us into agreement with their false world view and participate in their sinful rebellion. Since sin is so intimately connected with so much that we may say or do, including our emotional life, it is very easy to fall into the snare of looking at ourselves and others, seeing the sins and going into judgment. How does God keep His own great Heart clear of holding sins against us? If we can see from His perspective, we will see the way for our own hearts to live free of holding judgments. We have already seen that the Father's glory is His mercy and that He doesn't count our sins against us.[1] Now let us see the way that He looks upon us.

God Sees Us Differently Than We Do

Our loving God actually sees us as separate from our sins.[2] This is due to the great act of deliverance He accomplished for us when we were born again—He justified us freely in the Beloved giving us an entirely new righteous status based upon Jesus' death for our sins.[3] We asked Him to separate us from our sins and He did! He can see sin in us all day long and still see the person we are as separate from those sins—even sins of attitude and emotion, even the desire to sin that dwells so powerfully in us at times. Just consider what Paul is seeking to express:

> **Now if I do what I do not want, I agree with the law, that it is good. So now it is no longer I who do it, but <u>sin that dwells within me</u>. For I know that nothing good dwells in me, that is, in my flesh. For I have the desire to do what is right, but not the ability to carry it out. For I do not do the good I want, but the evil I do not want is what I keep on doing. Now if I do what I do not want, it is no longer I who do it, but <u>sin that dwells within me</u>.** Romans 7:16-20

Whenever scripture, like a parent, repeats something, we need to pay attention. Paul states it twice: "It is no longer I who do it, but sin that dwells in me." This is not Flip Wilson saying, "The devil made me do it." We are not being asked to abandon our responsibility for sin being in us, but we are being shown from heaven's perspective that *we are not our sins*, no *living* human is. The enemy and his kingdom have indeed become their sins, with no possibility of (or desire for) repentance and separation from them. Tragically those who never repent, the unredeemed who die in their sins, cannot be separated from them and end by being made one with their sins in hell. They actually become beings of sin. But we can be separated from our sins and can repent. The very fact that we repent of sin shows that it is a foreign invader in our lives—it is not who we really are. Never bind anyone to their sins. Right up to the moment of death it is possible for absolutely anyone to seek God for mercy and be set free from indwelling sin.

God has perfect vision. He can see every moment in time at all times. He is able to look upon us and always keep in mind three things about us: 1) the unseen past—who He created us to be, 2) the veiled future—who we will be in heaven and 3) the hidden present—who we really are even now deep down in Christ. He fashioned us in our mother's womb and He knew us before time began.[4] Since He is not the author of sin in us, His perfect vision still holds the image of who we really are before the fallen nature got attached to us and before generational sins or our own wrong choices began to have their effect. Not only that, but our Redeemer has 20/20 future vision and can always see who we are being redeemed to become as He draws us out of darkness into His light through the sanctifying work of the Spirit and our own belief in the truth.[5] But His vision extends beyond the past and our future; it sees deep within that there is a New Creation in us. He knows (and wants us to know) that this is who we really are now despite any stubborn, temporary agreements we may have with sin. We are not the old nature, we are not our sins and we are not our negative emotions. We are a New Creation!

> **Therefore if any person is** [ingrafted] **in Christ (the Messiah) he is a new creation (a new creature altogether); the old** [previous moral and spiritual condition] **has passed away. Behold, the fresh** *and* **new has come!** 2 Corinthians 5:17 AMP

Why Is This So Hard To Get?

Throughout the creation process, God declared that everything He was making was good. With Adam, however, God went even further. He said that Adam was "very good."[6] Keep this well in mind: All that God put into you is very good: your mind, your heart, your body, your renewed spirit. You are very good! However, when we allow sin to encroach upon our thoughts, words and deeds we are bringing in a foreign element, something God never put into us when He created us in our mother's womb. Three times in scripture we are shown how the Lord sees us as separate from the sin that dwells in us. The first was God questioning Adam about who he was "listening" to in the Garden.[7] The second time was Jesus rebuking Satan from speaking through Peter.[8] The third time came when Jesus rebuked the "sons of thunder" for wanting to call fire down on a village that had rejected Him.

> But the Lord God called to the man and said to him, "Where are you?" And he said, "I heard the sound of you in the garden, and I was afraid, because I was naked, and I hid myself." He said, "Who told you that you were naked?" Genesis 3:9-11

> But he turned and said to Peter, "Get behind me, Satan! You are a hindrance to me. For you are not setting your mind on the things of God, but on the things of man." Matthew 16:23

> But he turned and rebuked them, "You don't know of what kind of spirit you are." Luke 9:55 WEB

Like Adam and Peter, James and John, we may not even be aware that some of our "best" thinking is actually coming from the enemy—disguised as our own ideas and reasoning process. None of them were possessed, but they were giving ear to the enemy and voicing his perspective. Discern the voices: Who am I listening to and letting speak through me? Beware of "stinking thinking."

The real you is somebody both you and God want you to be. He is simply redeeming you to become who He created you to be. He didn't give you a sin nature or any of your patterns that don't match up with Jesus. That was Satan's way of "unmaking" you. God always sees the difference and we can learn to do it too. Grow spiritual eyes to see yourself and others as separate from whatever sins may be present. Because of the reconciliation won for us by Christ, God does not separate Himself from us—only from our sins. Our sins break our fellowship with Him—not His with us.[9] Therefore, we can confidently go to God with our sin still clinging to us, knowing by faith that He will love us and help us. In His eyes we who believe in Christ are always "covered" and protected by the Blood of Jesus, even when our need to be "cleansed" by the Blood is at its greatest. This is why He tells us to be bold in coming—He knows that many times we will have to come "slimed" by sin and need to be cleaned up on arrival!

> **Let us then with confidence draw near to the throne of grace, that we may receive mercy and find grace to help in time of need.**
> Hebrews 4:16

Deception Is Very Deceiving

The reason we need so much cleansing is due to the way that the "law of sin" wars within us against the new law of Christ.[10] This law of sin is the often unrecognized teaching of Satan in us which seems like obvious truth.[11] For example, it was the devil who "fathered" us into the idea that holding on to bitterness is better than letting go or that being anxious is better than trusting God. The truth is that everyone who sins has been blinded and deceived by an enemy. In compassion God "grants" repentance so that we may know the truth, come to our senses and separate ourselves from our sins and the enemy's snares with God's help. Let this grow mercy in you for others.

> **The Lord's servant must not quarrel, but be gentle towards all, able to teach, patient, in gentleness correcting those who oppose him: perhaps God may give them repentance leading to a full knowledge of the truth, and they may recover themselves out of the devil's snare, having been taken captive by him to his will.** 2 Timothy 2:24-26 WEB

One goal of effective spiritual warfare is to expose the real enemy, to reveal the true battleground. The real enemy is not your body, not the disease, not the depression, not the addiction, not the people who may have harmed you, not the people who led you astray. The real enemies are those spiritual powers of darkness whose thoughts masquerade as our own in order to tempt us to think, speak and act to serve their purposes. When we let sinful thoughts, attitudes and feelings dwell in us we are actually fellowshipping with evil beings and establishing Satan's kingdom on earth by doing his will instead of God's. By forgiving everyone (ourselves included) we shift the ultimate blame for evil to the demons who carried people captive into sin in the first place. We can then focus our righteous indignation on the enemy and his kingdom, where God keeps His anger and wrath focused. Certainly Jesus hates the wickedness of the enemy's kingdom.

> **You have loved righteousness and hated wickedness. Therefore God, your God, has anointed you with the oil of gladness beyond your companions.** Psalms 45:7

We, too, need to develop a perfect hatred for sin as the Psalmist did, and yet remember who the real enemy is under the conditions of our New Covenant. Shift the hate and blame from people to the one who enslaves them to do his will.[12]

> **Do I not hate those who hate you, O Lord? And do I not loathe those who rise up against you? I hate them with complete hatred; I count them my enemies.** Psalms 139:21-22

When we refuse to forgive someone as the law of Christ commands, we are saying to Jesus: "I don't believe your law is right. I believe my law of bitterness is better." God may well ask of us as He did of Adam, "Who told you that?" Through intercession and forgiveness we are to loose people from their sins and bind the real enemy. But when we bind people to their sins, we loose the enemy instead. Remember, we do not wrestle against flesh and blood, but against the invisible powers of evil.[13] Stay focused. Love God, love people and hate the real enemy!

> **For we do not wrestle against flesh and blood, but against the rulers, against the authorities, against the cosmic powers over this present darkness, against the spiritual forces of evil in the heavenly places.** Ephesians 6:12

Recognize, Discern, Separate!

Cultivating a perspective of separating people from their sins is a process of discernment and recognition—and the best person on which to practice this is yourself. Learn to notice the presence of negative emotions and wrong attitudes—these are not coming from your true self. Any loss of peace should alert you. Separate yourself from what is not like Christ in you. The good comes from the New Creation that you already are and are becoming.[14] The evil comes from the enemy. Stay in agreement with God and not the devil about who you are. As you learn to practice this with yourself, you will be much better equipped to cover others with the same grace. Once mastering this, you will learn to see everyone as separate from their sins—including yourself. Heaven's perspective is so much better than that of earth, for once you catch on to it you have to admit that it's, well, *heavenly…*

Father, forgive me for binding people to their sins and holding their sins against them. I repent of and renounce any deeply held belief that this is what You do. I confess that the truth is that You see us all as separate from our sins and can separate anyone from their sins who repents, including myself. Jesus, help me to join You as an intercessor for—not a judge of—myself and my fellow sinners.

CHAPTER 6

THE PATHWAY OF TEMPTATION

How is it that we so often fall into sin? Ever since the Fall sinning comes naturally to us. We don't have to *work* at being sinners! We can fall into sin without any effort at all because we already have a fallen nature ready to go in that direction. But there is someone who delights in tripping us up. Satan and his kingdom seek to make us fall by presenting us with deceptive temptations.[1]

For this reason, when I could bear it no longer, I sent to learn about your faith, for fear that somehow the tempter had tempted you and our labor would be in vain. 1 Thessalonians 3:5

The heart of the issue of temptation is this: Will we use our wills to agree with the enemy or with God about what is right to believe and to do? Naturally, we want to agree with God, but the enemy is a deceiver and he has had a lot of practice at making the wrong thing seem right and the right thing seem wrong. If he simply came out in the open and said, "My ways are guaranteed to kill you!" we would all turn away and run to God. Instead he twists the truth enough to make his perspective seem plausible and his paths seem desirable—all the while seeking to set his hook into our flesh. Note this about the following seven steps: Before sin ever becomes a struggle in our flesh, it has to gain *the agreement of our will*. To sin or not to sin is essentially a truth encounter, not a will power contest.

The Sin Process According to James

Let's learn to recognize and avoid these seven deadly stages of the sin process that James warns us about:[2]

Let no man say when he is tempted, "I am tempted by God," for God can't be tempted by evil, and he himself tempts no one. But each one is (1) tempted, when he is (2) drawn away (3) by his own lust, and (4) enticed. Then the lust, when it (5) has conceived, (6) bears sin; and the sin, when it is full grown, (7) brings forth death. Don't be deceived, my beloved brothers. James 1:13-16 WEB

Stage 1: Tempted

Temptation begins with the enemy, not you. Images, impulses or ideas that tempt us do not come from God or our flesh, but from Satan's kingdom. Some tempting impression is made upon the mind or heart by an evil spirit. At this point it is not sin, only a temptation to sin. Jesus was tempted in every way we are—so don't take on condemnation for being tempted.[3] You are being probed by an evil spirit to see if you will agree with it. Usually you will sense something in you shift as your attention is caught by the tempting thought. If the tempting impression is recognized for what it is and rejected out of hand, it ends there. But if the idea is entertained and in some way accepted, then the struggle begins. As Martin Luther once said of temptation, "You can't help it if a bird flies over your head, but you can stop it from building a nest in your hair."[4] Be asking: Whose voice is it? Mine? Or the enemy's!

There is a very real difference between being tempted and actually sinning—temptation is not the same thing as sinning no matter how strong or wrong it feels. Resist the devil and you may suddenly have a whale of a fight on your hands, but you are still on the right side of the issue. Coming into agreement with the tempting thought and doing what it desires is where the sin lies. Being assailed by tempting thoughts, however strongly they may be tugging at you through your wrong desires, is not sin. In the Garden of Gethsemane Jesus sweated blood in His effort to resist the temptation to avoid the cross, and He remained without sin despite the awful power of the enemy working upon Him. So resist all self-condemnation! Getting us to condemn ourselves for being tempted by him is very much a part of the enemy's game plan and it only makes it harder to fight back. Stay encouraged in the Lord— He sees your efforts to resist the snare. He knows your heart and does not condemn you.[5]

Stage 2: Drawn Away

Many think that the enemy's primary objective is to get us to sin, but the great issue of temptation is not what we are drawn *into* (sin), but what we are drawn *away from* (the Lord). Entertaining the evil thought draws us away from the peace and confidence that comes to us as we trust and obey our God. The enemy ever seeks to disconnect us from our source of strength and new life—for it is only in Christ that we are a threat to his kingdom.[6] Hence he wants to separate us from heart-peace and trust and then make it seem that such a life of surrender is undesirable or impossible. Even one small step away from being fully surrendered to the Lord is a step in the enemy's direction. The first task of resisting temptation is to reconnect with God and His grace. You know you have been "drawn away" if someone asks you how you are doing and you hear yourself say, "I'm just hanging in there." Hanging in there means, "I am still struggling and trying to be faithful, but it's killing me!" This beats giving up and going back, but it is a far cry from living in the grace that is offered us. On the other hand, if a person is fully surrendered, you usually don't have to ask how they are doing—it shines with a glow all over their face.

Stage 3: By His Own Lust

As temptation increases wrong desires begin to awaken out of the fallen nature. The old you comes back to life, sometimes with a vengeance. When the temptation finds a hook into a wrong desire ("lust" means *any* strong, but wrong desire, not just a sexually immoral one), formerly crucified feelings can sometimes spring back to life in an instant. Don't panic! Before that moment of temptation those feelings had been lying in the grave with the old you, and they will do so again as soon as you get your focus back on Christ. Jesus said the enemy had "nothing" in Him.[7] We should seek to be the same way by quickly reconnecting with God and His grace, then holding the wrong desire as a captive to His light until we see something in Him that makes it lose its emotional power.

Stage 4: Enticed

Enticed means to catch by using bait. At this point in the process we have already begun buying into some lie that the temptation represents—that's the bait. *Find the lie and break off the hook!* Otherwise, our will becomes "hooked" by agreeing with that deceptive thought, and negative emotions gain strength to overpower us. The evil spirit can only succeed if it breaks our agreement with God by getting us to agree instead with its own false and distorted belief system (see Chapter 4).

Stage 5: Conceived

Enticement generates a desire to give up the struggle by yielding our will to the enemy. We now want to give in to the temptation more than to resist it. Once such an agreement with sin is made (conceived), the actual sin (of thought, word or deed) is sure to follow. Once we have embraced a tempting thought by giving our heart to it, the temptation has become our sin.

> **But I say to you that everyone who looks at a woman with lustful intent has already committed adultery with her <u>in his heart</u>.**
> Matthew 5:28

Stage 6: Bears Sin

Now that the temptation is "treasured" in the heart it has become a sinful thing inside of us.[8] By our thoughts, words and deeds it is "birthed" as an expression of sin into the world.

Stage 7: Brings Forth Death

The sin, if it is un-repented, continues to kill and destroy that which the enemy attacks through it—especially our relationships of trust and love with God, self or others. Sin always works to produce death: first within the soul of the one who sins and then into the world around. We have become a servant of the enemy in that area of our life and reap accordingly.[9]

This whole process can take months, days, or fractions of a second. It can be stopped at any point, but it is easiest to stop in the early stages. The more frequently we give way the more likely it is that we will become enslaved. What began as a seemingly random temptation in a "weak" moment may well become a habit that is very hard to break. Such bondage—not being able to say no—indicates that we have given ourselves as *slaves* to sin.[10]

For just as you once presented your members as slaves to impurity and to lawlessness leading to more lawlessness, so now present your members as slaves to righteousness leading to sanctification.
Romans 6:19

Gaining Victory

Temptation is a lie of the enemy knocking on the door of your mind, seeking entrance to your heart. Capture the thought when it first starts knocking and carry it captive to Christ before it carries you captive to what the enemy wants you doing. Be on guard and get to it first. Then, reconnect quickly with God and His grace!

For the weapons of our warfare are not of the flesh, but mighty before God to the throwing down of strongholds, throwing down imaginations and every high thing that is exalted against the knowledge of God, and bringing every thought into captivity to the obedience of Christ. 2 Corinthians 10:4-5 WEB

Even temptation has a redemptive purpose, once we learn to recognize and resist it. God desires to move us from holy innocence to mature holiness by means of choice—maturing us through a growth process of sanctification that preserves and enhances our freedom of will.[11] God allows evil spirits to tempt us so that we can learn to discern good and evil, believe that His Word is the truth and rely completely on Him.[12] Whenever we fall, we can still choose to repent, return to God and learn to walk in His ways.

For the righteous falls seven times and rises again, but the wicked stumble in times of calamity. Proverbs 24:16

Let us remember that Jesus was tempted in every way just as we are, yet did not sin. There is hope for us in this, because Jesus defeated Satan's temptations as a man, in His full humanity. This is evident because the scripture says that "God cannot be tempted"—so it cannot be that Jesus was tempted in His divine nature.[13] And yet the Word also says that Jesus was tempted just as we are.[14] By this we see that Jesus, in His humanity, was tempted in *exactly* the same way that we are—by enticements coming from the enemy intended to deceive Him into giving sin a place within Himself.

Jesus, being conceived of the Holy Spirit and sinless, had no place within Him that was attracted to sin. He also was fully connected *by faith* to the Father's love, grace and truth and wasn't about to let anything disconnect Him. As reborn believers we, too, through the Holy Spirit have a new nature (at the core of our being) that is not attracted to sin and now enjoy a new connection to God through faith in Christ that we are meant to fight to maintain. The way that Jesus resisted temptation in His humanity, shows us the way we need to learn in order to effectively resist temptations. Jesus resisted temptations by resolutely holding fast to the truth of God's Word—and by carrying the enemy's lies captive to the Word.

> **Then Jesus said to him, "Be gone, Satan! For it is written, 'You shall worship the Lord your God and him only shall you serve.'" Then the devil left him, and behold, angels came and were ministering to him.** Matthew 4:10-11

As soon as you realize that temptation is seeking to disconnect you, fight the good fight of faith to get firmly reconnected with God's grace and His truth!

Father, the foremost temptation I will need to overcome is that of living by trusting and obeying myself, rather than You. Help me turn my life around! Make me willing to be made willing to surrender everything to You. According to Your love and wisdom, send whatever You desire to send of Your grace and blessings, allow whatever You have to allow of free will and its consequences, ask of me whatever You desire or require of inward and outward obedience, withhold me from and withhold from me whatever is necessary to fulfill Your plans. Help me to fully trust that You are working in and through all things for my good and Your glory. Then strengthen me to say in the midst of all temptations, "Not my will, but Yours be done."

CHAPTER 7

RECOGNIZE AND REPLACE!

In the previous chapter we explored the seven stages of temptation, noting that the enemy's primary objective is to draw us away from our rightful place of surrender and union with Christ. Since our salvation—in all of its forms—comes to us by grace *through faith* the center point of the enemy's attack quite naturally is to disconnect us from trusting in and relying upon our God and His grace. As soon as a potential disconnect begins, we start losing the peace of Christ which is meant to rule in our hearts *at all times*.[1] This loss of peace is the Holy Spirit "throwing a flag on the play," alerting us that we are being drawn in the wrong direction. Noticing that loss of peace—and understanding what it means— gives us a choice: We can choose life by seeking to reconnect with our source of new life (Jesus) or we can choose death by continuing to let the temptation gain ground within us.

Every fresh challenge or temptation, therefore, presents us with daily opportunities to grow spiritually *into Christ* or to fall back in reliance *upon Self*—our old nemesis and former god. Remembering this, recognizing the opportunity and taking advantage of it means that we need some principle of simplicity by which to ingrain the new ways. We call ours: *recognize and replace!* You have an enemy actively "seeking whom he may devour"—always wanting to separate you from your God and His ways by breaking the trust connection or detouring your path of obedience.[2] If you don't want to be robbed of your sweet surrender and the sense of peace and confidence it gives you, what can you do? *Recognize and replace!* Recognize that the emotions stealing over you are not coming from Christ in you and replace them with the emotional life Jesus desires you to have. For this you will often need to act fast to reconnect. Although difficult at first, eventually, the way of replacing our junk (past issues and present negative emotions) with His grace will become as practiced as riding a bicycle with no hands.

Here is an example of a typical episode involving the sudden appearance of negative emotions: The peace of Christ is given to you as you surrender, trust and follow Jesus. So now you feel confident in God and are *flowing in the river of peace, flowing in the river of peace, flowing in the river of peace.* But wait: A challenge just came to the flow! Interruption of peace! Alert! Battle stations! Something has come up *in* you or come down *on* you so that your peace is gone. You either have to deal with it or you will run from it; fight your way through it or surrender to it. Don't be passive! The enemy will use that to drag you down further. You are under attack, so *A.C.T.!* fast to reconnect.

A.C.T.! Fast to Reconnect

A) Admit: Admit right up front that you need help handling the situation or your emotions. That's why you feel weak and want to run, or hurt and want to lash out. Alone you are powerless to get the victories you need. The devil knows it. God knows it. So admit that you really do need God to be helping you *right now* with this situation, with your feelings, with your attitudes and desires—so that His peace can be restored.

C) Call: Call on Him! All who call on the Name of the Lord *will* be saved,[3] so start praying like your life depends upon it! Call for help, confess your need, come clean about any sin and cast that care on Him. You need His help right now, so ask, seek and knock. He is eager to help you, but you have to ask Him in—it's a free will issue. Has your sense of failure or moral weakness got you feeling condemned, unworthy? *Don't hold back.* Go boldly to His throne of grace anyway.[4] That's exactly what He wants you to do—to receive the mercy and help you need.

T) Trust: Trust yourself to God by laying hold of some lifesaving promise that offers you help and hope for this situation. Hold on tight to the truth of the promise. All kinds of good things are promised to you but you have to learn how to hold on to the truth of the promises when your emotions are under attack. You are separated from His peace and from seeing the way through, which is why you have to learn to live in the meantime by relying on His promises. Grab one or both of these: "I will never leave you or forsake you;" "No weapon formed against you will prosper." Put it in first person: "All things are being made to work for my good;" "Not even this can separate me from my Father's love." Bet your life on it! *Our new life is lived out in this Land of Promises!*

A.C.T.) Act: Put steps A, C, T together *and act*. Don't be passive—this is war! Obey whatever it is that you honestly believe the Lord wants you to do. Sometimes it is just "be still and wait." At other times it may be "deny yourself and take up this cross" (do the very thing you don't want to do). Or it may be something easy or unexpected that the Spirit will show you. Stay open but *be ready to act as soon as that idea takes shape.* Learning to obey Jesus is the new way of life that leads to fullness of joy. Step out in His direction!

!) Thank Him: Begin thanking Him even before you see *His action* coming your way. Thank Him that His promises are true. Thank Him that He is teaching you to trust His promises. Thank Him that you can come so quickly to His throne of grace, that He reminded you to call on His Name and helped you to do it. Thank Him and praise Him that what the enemy meant for evil (in seeking to disconnect you from God and His peace), He is now using (through *your ACT-ions*) to reconnect you.

Now peace is restored! The peace of Christ is given to you as you surrender, trust and follow Jesus. Once again you are *flowing in the river of peace, flowing in the river of peace, flowing in the river of peace.* But wait: A challenge just came up! Here we go again...

Dislodging a Stronghold: The 6 R's

There may be a further problem, however, if the disconnect is happening in an un-mended area of your life where you have never experienced much of a "reconnect." If you have never yet known the peace or the victory of Christ in that area of your life, then you may need a deeper work in order to get a breakthrough over the power of that stronghold. A.C.T.!-ing fast to reconnect is intended to give you quicker victories over negative emotions in the midst of normal life. This is a powerful way to achieve mastery over your inner state so that you can stay connected to Christ and *keep the river flowing*. But what if that particular river has never flowed properly for you? What if you need recovery and restoration of your emotional state from unresolved past issues before you can practice mastery?

The following six steps to freedom will help you return to walking in the light.[5] If you are stuck in a pattern and want to get free of it, you may need to break up what is now a hard work of repentance into these easier to understand steps. You may need to practice these six steps very deliberately *at first* in order to get effective victories in the stronghold areas that we will be exploring in later chapters. As toddlers we all had to learn to walk in the natural; these are spiritual "baby steps" which will help you walk in the Spirit in areas where you still need restoration and recovery.

1) Recognize: Unless you can see that *your way* is amiss then there is no way to get back on track. Let the Holy Spirit turn on the lights, showing you by a loss of peace that there has been a loss of trust or obedience on your part. Learn to discern where sinful attitudes have taken over. Separate yourself from what is not you. The good is Christ *in you*—that's your core. The rest comes from the enemy. If it is not of God, it is not the real you (see Chapter 9). *That wrong thing in you* (fearfulness, jealousy, shyness, etc.) *is not you.* Notice what it sounds like (its message) and what it feels like (its pressure) when it goes off inside you. It may have been "a part" of you for so long that it seems like it is just the way you are, but it isn't. Somewhere along the way *it came inside from the outside.* Break all agreements with the enemy and repent of any sinful reactions to originating events you may have had. *Rightly recognizing sin as sin* (that it is not good, not you and that it has to go) is half the battle.[6]

2) Responsibility: Own it. Take responsibility for your part in it. Others may have sinned against you, but how you reacted to what they did is *fully* your responsibility. Allow yourself no excuses, no avoidance and no denial—repent of every attitude and action that missed the mark. True maturity is accepting and taking responsibility for what you recognize in you *that is not of God.* If it got in, you let it in or kept it in—stop blaming others. Don't look for a way out: Face it. Taking responsibility enables

you to confess and repent honestly to God and to acknowledge that He is right, rather than seeking to vindicate your ways.[7]

Taking responsibility restores you to being the true sovereign over your own heart and will. Your emotional reactions are the result of your own deeply held beliefs about right and wrong ways of responding to what is going on around you. If you try to make other people responsible for what you feel and do, you will always be ruled by their words and actions. But you are the head and not the tail when it comes to your emotional life: You can carry any thought or emotion captive to Christ and you can repent of your ways and choose to believe in God's ways. Eventually this change in believing (when it goes deep enough) will bring about a shift in your emotional reactions in the future.[8] By submitting your emotional life to Christ He enables you to rule over it (see Negative Emotions in the Postscripts).

3) Return: Make a quick return to the Father. *Reconnect with His love and mercy.*[9] Some wrong turns were made inside your thought-life that carried you away from being fully trusting of His love or fully submitted to His ways, allowing the stronghold to form in you. Turn back to God and His ways now. Don't delay like the prodigal son did, fearing that he wouldn't be received in love. There is "a refreshing" promised to those who repent, for it leads to freedom once we turn and reconnect with God's grace.[10] Cast all your cares on Him!

4) Renounce: Fall totally out of agreement with the enemy: Declare sin to be sin; declare its half-truths to be total lies; declare God's truth to be truth; and declare yourself to be committed to God no matter what. Then keep confessing God's truth that counteracts the lies behind the sin you have been walking in. Cultivate a perfect hatred for that sin.[11] Make sin the enemy—not any person. Break agreement with anything that excuses or condones the sin. Discover and renounce the hidden lie the sin used to entice you, and confess the truth that God's Word declares. Carry every thought about it captive to Christ.[12]

5) Remove: If need be, have someone pray with you to cast out any spirit that is not removed through repentance.[13] Get rid of the things in your life that are causing you to sin.[14] Be aware of

this dynamic: If you want God, the Holy Spirit alerts you to dangers; if you want the sin, the enemy puts people and temptations in your path. Separate from "friends" who pull you down and away from Christ.

6) Resist: The spirit will try to come back and the stronghold will seek to reassert itself, so be prepared to keep resisting. Give the burden of the struggle to God. Don't try to strong arm it in your own strength. Run to Jesus instead. Draw near to Him first, then through His power and support, resist the temptations.[15] It takes time to break old mental habits and start new ones. Don't give up: perseverance always prevails![16]

Pray, Persevere and Press in!

Restoration takes time and many individual moments of repentance. Give yourself grace and work through these steps little by little. Let God reveal to you what you need to deal with and let Him set the pace. Be gentle on yourself. Be a friend to yourself. But be very courageous about facing the truth.[17] Being saved by God requires a love of the truth—over and above the love of Self. Without total honesty, openness and transparency about your sins and stronghold areas, repentance is shallow at best.

"Pressing in" to the Kingdom is when you exercise faith to believe for freedom even under attack and keep pressing forward to trust and obey as fully as you can. No matter how bad things are, no matter how badly you may seem to be doing, no matter how bad you feel you *always* have a God who loves you, has covered you with mercy, is working all things for your good and who deeply desires you to reconnect with Him. Return to Him first, refresh your heart with His love and mercy, and then receive the grace and strength to keep going.

Father, somehow I have lost the peace in this area of my life and can't seem to get it back. I need Your help! Forgive me and work with me to restore me to trust and obedience. I embrace what You have promised me in Your Word. Show me any steps I will need to take. Thank You for helping me learn to "guard my heart" and walk more closely with You.

SECTION TWO:
IMAGE BEARING

*But we all, with unveiled face beholding as in a mirror
the glory of the Lord, are transformed
into the same image from glory to glory,
even as from the Lord, the Spirit.*
2 Corinthians 3:18 WEB

CHAPTER 8

BEHOLDING THE TRUE IMAGE

In Chapter 7 we saw that the first step out of a stronghold depends upon recognition of sin and the second involves our willingness to take full responsibility for the sin we recognize. Both of these steps are directly impacted by the images that we carry in our heart of hearts. If we "see" that our true self looks like Jesus (His nature now in us as our new nature), then we will be able to discern that anything in us that doesn't look like Jesus must be coming from sin—*not our true self*. But we won't be able to see what God may want to show us or be willing to take much responsibility for sin that is in us if we are carrying a distorted image of the Father, making us want to run and hide from God in shame as Adam did.[1] In this chapter we will look into the all-important place that image-bearing holds for us. Then in the following two chapters we will study first our own image and then the Image of God the Father, as they are both now being restored to us through the revelation of Jesus Christ, the God-Man.

The Power of Beholding

Since our hearts have "eyes," we need to learn how to keep our inward focus on the Lord.[2] We have been warned, therefore, to be careful what we behold, because we inevitably become like what we behold. Consider the transformation that takes place on the countenance of women when they see a baby or on the faces of children when they watch a fireworks display. Now, recall how most folks look when they are worried about a problem: quite a difference! What gets our attention "gets us." As it gets us, it *transforms* us, thus the power of beholding. For this reason Israel was forbidden to create images to depict God, the second of the Ten Commandments.[3] Since, no created image can do justice to the true Image of the Creator, God didn't want His children beholding and thereby becoming like any false image of Him. They were specifically warned against bowing down to (worshipping) and serving false images.[4]

Worship, which means "to ascribe worth to," and service are intimately connected for we will serve throughout the day what our hearts are focused upon.[5] By "bearing" (or carrying deep within) what we behold, we then begin "birthing" that image into life—by our thoughts, words and deeds. We actually become like what we are worshipping—what we are focusing upon. We are made over into the image we bear in our heart of hearts; this applies both to the Image of God and to the image of man.

Any distortion of either image will hinder our walk and deplete our joy because emotions always tend to match up with what has our focus. Fortunately, we can get our emotions released by putting our focus back where it belongs—on the Lord. Just imagine how quickly your emotions would change if Jesus *visibly* showed up. Now, realize that *by faith* you can "see" Him at any time your believing matches your level of need—and get an emotional shift. Psychologists call the speed by which emotions shift when focus shifts, the "cascade effect."[6] Let it work for you! You get to choose to believe, see and be transformed—if you want to.

Beholding is Key to Our Transformation

This awesome power of beholding is what the Father is using to save and transform the world. Consider the following fourfold series of revelations designed to completely transform us. What changes us all along the way is not our work—our righteousness—but the grace of looking to Jesus and seeing in Him the answer to everything that is dark or needy in us. Let these truths propel you into a lifetime adventure of "getting the look that gives the shift."

1) Beholding Initiates Life

The revelation of Jesus Christ brings us into the Christian life. By the Fall we lost the capacity to behold our God. We became spiritually blind as our hearts were veiled.

And even if our gospel is veiled, it is veiled only to those who are perishing. In their case the god of this world has blinded the minds

of the unbelievers, to keep them from seeing the light of the gospel of the glory of Christ, who is the image of God. 2 Corinthians 4:3-5

With salvation we now behold Him with eyes of faith—as Jesus our Savior is revealed to us. This revelation ushers in the new birth.

He said to them, "But who do you say that I am?" Simon Peter replied, "You are the Christ, the Son of the living God." And Jesus answered him, "Blessed are you, Simon Bar-Jonah! For flesh and blood has not revealed this to you, but my Father who is in heaven." Matthew 16:15-17

But when he… was pleased to reveal his Son to me. Galatians 1:15-16

But I received it [his conversion] through a revelation of Jesus Christ. Galatians 1:12

2) Beholding Saves and Sustains

The revelation of Jesus Christ saves us and sustains us. We cannot live the Christian life in our own strength—looking to ourselves for the righteousness, wisdom, abilities or saving power we need. Calling upon the Lord in prayer is God's way of training us to behold Jesus, rather than some lesser source of help or hope, such as Self or others. We learn to look to Jesus every step of the way, seeking to see in Him something that we need to see in each moment of our need. Do you need forgiveness? Look to Jesus. Do you need wisdom? Look to Jesus. Do you need someone to carry your burdens? Look to Jesus. And keep looking until the concern is lifted. Faith looks through the veil and sees Him as He really is. Then believing becomes restored trust, and once restored, trust can become renewed obedience.[7]

Look to me, and be you saved, all the ends of the earth; for I am God, and there is none else. Isaiah 45:22 WEB

Let us run with endurance the race that is set before us, looking to Jesus, the founder and perfecter of our faith. Hebrews 12:1-2

3) Beholding Transforms and Sanctifies

The revelation of Jesus Christ transforms us in this life.[8] When we behold Him (even dimly) by faith, we bear His Image and begin to become like Him. The new nature which is Christ in us, or the life of the Spirit in us, comes to life whenever we look to Jesus and see something in Him that lets us surrender everything to Him. Until this happens and our trust and obedience are flowing freely again, we are still caught up in trying to live our lives *our* way. "Let go and let God" have His way and watch new life begin to flow. Whenever this happens, we are no longer "hanging in there" trying in our own strength to live the Christian life, we have surrendered, become transformed and the Holy Spirit is lifting us and carrying us. We have passed from "crucifixion" with Christ into resurrection.[9] Jesus begins living through us! This is the Spirit's work of raising us into the new life of grace whenever we get our focus and our faith restored.

Jesus' life comes into us when we are born again (as inward sight is given); His life flows out through us at any moment when we surrender everything to Him (as inward sight is restored). When we look to Him, we walk in the light whenever we see in Him something that enables us to trust and surrender. The old nature is laid to rest like a shadow behind us and we are released to walk by His Spirit.[10] That newer, better, more loving version of you comes forth and breathes the sweet air of freedom. This is the graceful transformation of our lives from the inside out which no work of the flesh can accomplish.[11] Religious practices and moral striving don't accomplish this—or we would have something to boast about.[12] The Spirit does it all—*as we behold Jesus.*

> **And we all, with unveiled face, beholding the glory of the Lord, are being transformed into the same image from one degree of glory to another. For this comes from the Lord who is the Spirit.**
> 2 Corinthians 3:18

> **And have put on the new self, which is being renewed in knowledge after the image of its creator.** Colossians 3:10

4) Beholding Glorifies

The revelation of Jesus Christ will complete our transformation in heaven. God will not have to change what he has already been doing to bring forth our new life there. In heaven sight will replace faith as the veil of time and space is forever lifted. We will clearly behold Jesus and instantly become just like Him! We will see Jesus in all His matchless glory and that will bring the new life in us fully into being. Our ultimate glorification flows out of the power released by fully beholding our glorious Lord.

As for me, I shall behold your face in righteousness; when I awake, I shall be satisfied with your likeness. Psalm 17:15

Beloved, we are God's children now, and what we will be has not yet appeared; but we know that when he appears we shall be like him, because we shall see him as he is. 1 John 3:2

Let us praise God for the power of beholding Jesus. Looking to Him we are saved "to the uttermost."[13] We call this pattern of losing spiritual sight and regaining it: "Eyes off? EYES ON!" Learn to "get the look that gives the shift"—and keep getting it!

Let Beholding Grow You

Even the five vital requirements for growth listed below do not automatically transform us. Every Christian needs to be actively cultivating all five of these God-given means of staying connected to Jesus, our Living Vine. Even so, we would be wise to understand that they are not foolproof or automatic ways of becoming like Christ. These necessary, very wholesome, elements of our discipleship can actually be used by the enemy to draw us away from our place of surrender into pride, complacency and self-righteousness. We can do these as ritual or routine—but beholding Jesus *through* them is what transforms us.

1) Bible study: The Pharisees knew the scriptures, but many couldn't recognize Him.

2) Prayer: The publican prayed even longer than the sinner, but left unchanged.

3) Worship: Lucifer led worship, but got his eyes on himself instead of Jesus.

4) Fellowship: Can be superficial or supernatural. Are you being honest, open, transparent?

5) Service: Can easily become a work of the flesh. We serve in Him, by Him and unto Him, not to meet our own needs.

Repent of and renounce any of the ways that these five disciplines may be building self-righteousness in you. Instead, seek to use each discipline as a way of making sure your inner focus is upon the Lord. Your peace and joy levels should be going up as you practice them, indicating that you are connecting with His grace and truth. Then pray for God to help you learn to guard the Image of God inside your heart that is being renewed within you.

Keep your heart with all diligence, for out of it is the wellspring of life. Proverbs 4:23 WEB

The Way of Restoration

Being restored to the life God intends for us to live depends upon recognizing when our inward focus has shifted away from beholding by faith the One whose image we were created to bear.

1) The first step of restoration is receiving a living faith in Jesus Christ—all else depends upon that!

2) The next is taking full responsibility for having built one's life around trusting and obeying Self, instead of Jesus: Repent and renounce all desire to live in rebellion, un-surrendered and un-submitted to His leadership. Let His peace fill your heart!

3) Turn to the Father and release gratitude for the grace-filled way He has of transforming us through beholding His Son!

Father, I renounce trying to change myself by my own efforts. Only by beholding Jesus am I actually transformed. Make me aware of those times when my heart turns away from beholding Him. Help me cast down all false images of myself, of others and of You. By Your grace make me willing to be made willing to surrender everything to You.

CHAPTER 9

OUR NEW IDENTITY

The all-important issue of identity determines so much about how we will live and what we will do with our time here on earth. No one who has a poor self-image can truly enjoy living, yet the gospel has not come to tell you how great you are. Jesus says: "Without me you can do nothing," and Paul writes, "For I know that in me (that is, in my flesh) nothing good dwells."[1] Hardly a formula for pride based self-esteem! So what is the answer to our identity questions? Discovering who we really are—now that Jesus has come to live inside of us. And our sense of self-worth? It is based upon the solid rock of His love for us. Period. You are *His beloved*—just try to wrap your heart around the enormity of that blazing truth. He lived and died and lives again to bring you fully to life. Everything else you could hope to get out of life—compared to this—is chump change.[2]

Identity and the Lost Image

What could be of more practical value to us than discovering who we really are? There are two great questions that challenge every human being: Is there a God and who am I? Socrates, after his encounter with the oracle of Delphi, believed he was commissioned by God to teach wisdom to men. The foundation of his teaching? *Know thyself.* Our fundamental problem is that we do not know who our God is; therefore, we do not know who we really are. We are suffering from a massive loss of identity made even worse by our failure to realize it and face up to it.

The fall from grace created our identity crisis. We tend to think mainly of the Fall as a fall into sin and into the sin nature, which it certainly was. We say rightly that fallen man, once created in the Image of God, no longer reflects that image. But one essential effect of the Fall was that, in dying spiritually, Adam could no longer behold his God. Both the Image of God and the image of man *fell* from his sight. Adam could neither see who God is nor could he see who he himself truly was, since who we are is entirely defined in relation to God who created us. Jesus has come to restore both our lost vision (see Chapter 8) and our true identity.

New Creations

Now that faith in Christ has come to us, we are New Creations. This is the miracle of new birth which raises us from our sin and separation from God into eternal life in union with our God.[3]

> **Therefore if anyone is in Christ, he is a new creation. The old things have passed away. Behold, all things have become new.**
> 2 Corinthians 5:17 WEB

What does it mean to be New Creations? We still see a lot of the old nature and the former ways of living, thinking and feeling, but new things have been added that radically change *all* things. However, before we look at the things that have become new, let's review what has not changed or passed away. Paul is not telling us that we no longer have a sin nature to contend with or sins to resist. Above all the apostles, he lays out the ongoing struggle between the New Creation (spirit) and the old nature (flesh) in texts too numerous to fully mention.[4] So what does pass away?

1) The person who did not know that Jesus is both Savior and Lord no longer exists. That person (your former self) has indeed passed away now that the revelation of Jesus Christ has come. If a blind person regains sight and sees the sun, even if the blindness returns, they will never be the same.

2) Before conversion, we were one with our sins. With our repentance and faith in Christ, the Father separated us from our sins by forgiving them and justifying us.[5] There is still an ongoing battle with sin, but continuing in sin is a spoiled thing for New Creations for two main reasons: one, the conviction of the Spirit; two, the sense of separation from Christ. Both overshadow the former pleasures of unrighteousness, enabling us to learn to hate sin. Many of our old ways, therefore, change with conversion, but not all. We are engaged in an all new process of ongoing conversion, which includes cleansing and growth in Christ.[6]

3) We are no longer "on the outside." We were formerly not a people, but now we are a part of God's family. We were strangers to the covenant, but now have been brought near, being made one with His Body on earth.[7]

This way of seeing the new birth (by what passed away) is like looking in the rear view mirror while driving. The really stunning, forward-looking view is how we now appear as New Creations!

- We have been spiritually reborn through the revelation of Jesus Christ (Chapter 8).
- We can no longer measure anything without reference to Christ.[8]
- We have been given a new heart and new spirit—a new nature![9]
- We live under a new covenant of immense mercy.[10]
- We are given the Holy Spirit, the righteousness of Christ and the Name of Jesus.
- We are not our past, not our sin, not our negative emotions—we are New Creations!

We are also a mystery even to ourselves. God is bestowing a new identity upon us only He knows. Who we now are is only revealed whenever we trust and obey Jesus—we are "hidden" in Him. He is the key! As we die to Self (the false god), we live through trusting and obeying Jesus.[11]

For you have died, and your life is hidden with Christ in God. Colossians 3:3

Then Jesus told his disciples, "If anyone would come after me, let him deny himself and take up his cross and follow me." Matthew 16:24

Our acceptance by God as New Creations is absolute, complete and unwavering. Try to fathom the massive liberation that God has accomplished by the Blood of atonement, our new covering.

It was God...in Christ, reconciling *and* restoring the world to favor with Himself, not counting up *and* holding against [men] their trespasses [but cancelling them]. 2 Corinthians 5:19 AMP

This incredible Reconciliation covers all that we have been in Adam and will be in Christ. Faith is what God gives us so that we can receive this grace and be translated from the kingdom of darkness (in Adam) to the Kingdom of His Son (in Christ), but faith did not in any way change God's Heart towards us, which is love, or His reconciliation to our sins, which Jesus accomplished fully at the cross. In conversion the former self (that had no life in Christ) passed away and the true self (that lives through trusting Christ) has been reborn/regenerated. The New Creation is a redeeming of the old, not an elimination of all that was former. We have a fresh start and a new center from which to live at any moment.

We Are New, But the Old Is in Us

The New Creation "comes to life" in us whenever we trust in the One who is our new life. As we "walk in the light" trusting God through Jesus Christ, our old nature is laid to rest like a shadow lying down behind us.[12] However, the one Paul calls "the old man" wants back in. Our old nature "comes back to life" in us whenever we cease to rely upon our God. Are we going to live by a resuscitation of the old self, or by a resurrection of the new life? The choice is ever before us.

> **I have been crucified with Christ... it is no longer I who live, but Christ... lives in me; and the life I now live in the body I live by faith in (by adherence to and reliance on and complete trust in) the Son of God, Who loved me and gave Himself up for me.** Galatians 2:20 AMP

The old nature draws power from false ideas of self shaped by the world. Some of us carry elements in our personality that we think of as ourselves. They are in us—but not us!

Nervous energy/anxious feelings	Deep wellsprings of grief
Perfectionism (people pleasing)	Feelings of persistent loneliness
Addictions/compulsions	Depression, heaviness of heart
Drive to achieve (self-salvation)	Nuclear reactivity/panic mode
Flashes of anger (hot temper)	Impatience (prickly, irritable)
Excessive sensitivity (easily hurt)	Stubbornness (pride, rebellion)
Timidity/shyness (fear of man)	Impulse to control/be in control

These ideas of self are not who we really are! Any or all of these may describe our personality as we have known it until now, but they are not our true God-given personhood. They reveal where the fallen nature still has power to block the life of the New Creation from coming forth, but they tell us nothing of what the Father created us to be before the enemy began "unmaking" us. Consider these two things about our "personalities":

1) In the womb these negative traits weren't in us. Even as young children we trusted and loved freely—no baggage!

2) When we die and go to heaven, these traits will have to be removed from us. They are not God's desire for us.

Restoration of our true life begins by breaking agreement with false beliefs about ourselves and choosing instead to embrace what God is speaking to us about our new identity. Two images fell when Adam fell—that of God and that of us. Get your image rightly set by seeing His. Whatever does not look like Jesus in you, isn't the real you. Refuse to be deceived by your enemy about who you really are. Apply the six steps to freedom in Chapter 7! Never settle for anything less than "Christ in you, the hope of glory."[1] Proper self-love is accepting God's view of us—it is not pride, false humility, or self-absorption. Let's get purified from all false ideas of ourselves.[2]

The Great Exchange

Apart from Christ we will be weak, foolish, sinful and ignorant in many ways, but in Christ we are complete, secure and sustained by His life. As Archbishop François Fénelon wrote, "Expect nothing of yourself, but all things of God. Knowledge of one's own hopeless, incorrigible weakness combined with absolute confidence in God's power are the two foundations of the spiritual life."[3] God is not asking us to perfect or change ourselves, but to turn to Him and learn to see and believe all of life from His perspective. Heaven's perspective on our life is always liberating. Take a moment to "look through" to heaven with your eyes of faith and seek to catch a glimpse of who you are in your eternal being. This is the real you—the eternal you. Then let the power of that glorious vision be released with "prophetic decree" into your own heart *now*. If you are in Christ, then read and confess with full faith:

- I am eternally the beloved bride of my Savior Jesus.
- I am eternally a receiver of God's love, mercy, wisdom, saving help and never-ending life.
- I am only a sinner needing mercy for a short while on earth.
- I am in Christ and He is in me—forever!
- I am an eternal being with a spirit as free as the wind and a soul of dazzling beauty and grace.
- I am indestructible in my being, due to His life in me.
- I am worse in my fallen-ness and better in my new created-ness than I ever imagined.

The Way of Restoration

Joy is produced in us whenever we realize by an active faith who we really are in Him. Even so, the truly great joy is not who we are in Christ, but who He is to us!

1) Learn to recognize all false images of self that don't match up with Jesus and which block your new life from coming forth.

2) Take full responsibility for your attachment to these false ideas of self: Repent, renounce and break all agreement with the enemy about who you are, confessing the truth instead.

3) Turn to the Father and release gratitude that who you are in Christ already looks a lot like Him—you are a New Creation!

Father, as a New Creation I cannot define myself by anything less than who I now am in Christ without damaging my self-image, security, sense of worth and purpose. I will therefore accept no lesser definitions of who I am. Help me break all agreement with my former ways of seeing myself and trust completely in Your heavenly perspective!

CHAPTER 10

THE FATHER'S HEART OF LOVE

In the previous chapter we looked at how Jesus is restoring to us the lost vision of our true humanity. We saw that the image of ourselves we carry in our hearts must match up with who we are as New Creations remade in His Image, or we will unwittingly block our own growth with false understandings of who we are. Here is another marvel: Jesus, because He is fully human *and* fully divine, also restores to us a true Image of what our Father is really like. All false images of ourselves and of our God are alike demolished and replaced by looking to Jesus! It is an incredible thing that God can restore these two glorious images, once lost and broken through the Fall, by means of revealing the God-Man, our Lord Jesus Christ.

The Danger of a Distorted Image

We have been created in God's Image to be *bearers* of His Image—not just to reflect His Image. Image is everything in the spiritual life. Not the image we can recite, but the image we "bear" or carry deep within our heart. The image we hold of God the Father hidden away in our heart of hearts will determine: how we will seek the Father; how we will respond to what He allows in our lives; how we will act towards others. Jesus kept His spiritual eyes constantly focused upon a true vision of the Father. All that He did flowed out of that ongoing faith connection.[1] This is the all-essential matter of keeping the heart rightly set.[2] Unfortunately, the idea we have of Father God is often misshaped by Adam's nature, earthly fathers and church tradition. It can be a fallen image buried in our heart distorting the true Image. Consider the powerful influence of these three image shapers:

1) Adam's nature is in us, still seeking to hide from God in guilt and fear of punishment, ashamed of our sinful "nakedness."

2) Our birth fathers (and mothers) may have been uncaring, distant, over-bearing, unaffectionate, abusive, threatening, harsh

in discipline, angry in punishment, and sinful—creating powerful, but false impressions of what God the Father is like.

3) Our spiritual fathers (and mothers), even beloved pastors and teachers may have planted wrong images of the Father as being different from Jesus in His ways with us—less loving, more judgmental, easily offended, stern and strict.

None of these distorted images reveal Father God. They actually resemble the enemy instead. These false images must be cast down! We cast them down first by forgiving the ones who sowed distorted images in us, and then by renouncing the lies that were planted and confessing the truth in their place.

The Image Formed by Our Birth Family

Our fathers (and mothers) can contribute to a distorted image of Father God because they are as a god to us when we are little— teaching us right from wrong and exercising power over us. As children we are looking to see God in our fathers—all the more so since our hearts are blocked from knowing the heavenly Father's love and Presence by the sin nature. No earthly father entirely measures up, but a solid foundation of affection, love and proper discipline makes a huge difference in forming who we will become. The lack of this solid foundation leaves a void, often a hurting wound, which the enemy has many ways of poisoning. There are crucial things we all needed our fathers to say to us, but which many of us never heard: "I love you; You're a good child; I'm proud of you; I'm glad you were born."

Every home needs a godly father. Godly order in scripture shows us that the head of the woman is the man; the head of the man is Christ; the head of Christ is the Father.[3] The father sets the emotional tone of a household and provides the moral framework for living in the family. The first word babies often say is "dada." Children are left as "spiritual orphans" when father's are not covering their families with godly love and discipline.

Statistics give us a sense for the emotional and societal damage caused by failed fathering. In the USA over 90% of prisoners are males; 95% of those on death row hated their fathers.[4] Many prisoners don't even know who their fathers were. The "father wound" is pervasive and deadly. We all carry the "first father wound" stemming from Adam's sin. Many of us also bear the "birth father wound" from our parents, a "father in God wound" from our religious upbringing and a "father impostor wound" from the enemy's direct working. The "father wound" carries a societal curse—a heavy consequence "in the land." Small wonder that so much restoration is needed in our own day.

> **Behold, I will send you Elijah the prophet before the great and terrible day of Yahweh comes. He will turn the hearts of the fathers to the children, and the hearts of the children to their fathers, lest I come and strike the earth with a curse.** Malachi 4:5-6 WEB

Clarifying Our Image of the Father

In truth people often think they begin with knowing God the Father. Actually we only know *about* Him by name as Father God, but relate to Him more as "the great high God"—distant and unknowable until a living faith through Christ is birthed in us. Jesus came to reveal the Father personally and much more intimately as *Abba,* just as He also came to baptize us with the Holy Spirit. The order of the three great pilgrimage festivals that Israel was commanded to observe reveals spiritual realities about our new life in Christ which are very interesting. Passover came first in early spring, prefiguring Jesus the true Passover Lamb. Next came Pentecost in late spring, a celebration of the "early harvest," which exactly coincided with the outpouring of the Holy Spirit upon the Early Church. Finally, Tabernacles, the great Feast of Harvest, arrived at the end of summer after a long growth period. Drawing a Trinitarian analogy to the Festivals, Tabernacles, therefore, relates to the Father. An intimate relationship with the Father is not automatic—it often comes only after a long period of growth (if at all), but it is absolutely necessary for establishing our hearts in sufficient grace that we may dwell (tabernacle) with our God.

The revelation of the Father's glorious grace began in the Old Testament. God the Father revealed His glory—the glorious nature of His grace-filled Being—to Moses.

The Lord passed before him and proclaimed, "The Lord, the Lord, a God merciful and gracious, slow to anger, and abounding in steadfast love and faithfulness." Exodus 34:6

This is what Paul refers to when he tells us that our sins consist in falling short of God's glory.[5] Our selfish and unloving choices in no way reflect our Father's glorious ability to shower love and mercy, grace and goodness, upon the whole of His creation. So great is His glorious grace that our Father in heaven does not even hold our sins against us. He hates our sins and in His goodness will patiently work to bring us to repentance so that we can be separated from them, all the while maintaining a Spirit of reconciliation towards us in His great Heart.

It was God [personally present] in Christ, reconciling *and* restoring the world to favor with Himself, not counting up *and* holding against [men] their trespasses [but cancelling them], and committing to us the message of reconciliation (of the restoration to favor). 2 Corinthians 5:19 AMP

Our grace-filled Father affirmed His only begotten Son by expressing His love for Jesus in public displays of affection. There are three audible words of God which Jesus heard that are recorded for us in scripture. In all of them the true Father affirmed His Son: at His baptism, on the mount of transfiguration and before the cross.[6] Astoundingly, the Father has the same love for all who are in Christ by faith. If you are a believer, Father God desires to affirm and express His love to you. There is no one He loves more than you. There is no one He loves less than you—He doesn't play favorites. He loves us all as much as He loves Jesus! If this scripture fails to move your heart, pray for fresh grace to be amazed by the stunning implications of what Jesus is saying about the Father's love *for you*.

I in them and you in me, that they may become perfectly one, so that the world may know that you sent me and loved them even as you loved me. John 17:23

This is what our gracious Father is really like:

- The Father delights to give us the Kingdom.[7]

- The Father has no darkness about Him.[8]
- He is the giver of every good gift.[9]
- The Father disciplines only in love.[10]
- It is His goodness that draws us to repent.[11]
- The Father is unconditional love.[12]
- The Father completely accepts us.[13]
- He is reconciled to us the way we are.[14]
- He favors us with right standing in His sight.[15]
- Your Father has never been angry with you.[16]

Let Jesus Reveal the Father to You

Jesus came on a mission to reveal the Father and restore His true image to us. Both by His life and by His death His stated intention was to reveal the Father.

Philip said to him, "Lord, show us the Father, and it is enough for us." Jesus said to him, "Have I been with you so long, and you still do not know me, Philip? Whoever has seen me has seen the Father. How can you say, 'Show us the Father'? Do you not believe that I am in the Father and the Father is in me?" John 14:8-10

Here is the idea made simple: The Father is just like Jesus! The New Testament not only gives us permission, it makes it a requirement of faith that we cast down every image of the Father we may have been given that does not match up with Jesus.

I and the Father are one. John 10:30

If this is who God really is to you and for you (and it is), then actually knowing and believing it will produce joy and peace in you and love through you in any moment of your life in which you touch this living reality by faith.[17] Active, believing faith always has that kind of power. Faith is what puts us in touch with *reality*. Not to live in a faith like this is to live a bad dream from which One Day we will all be awakened in His Presence. Why not awaken now?

As we behold the true image of the Father our hearts become established. So let us learn to run to "Home Base." Begin each day intentionally checking to see if your heart really believes these five great liberating truths about God the Father. Your Father is always:

1) Loving you—with full warmth of affection (John 17:23).

2) Forgiving you—with overflowing mercy (Hebrews 4:16).

3) Saving you—eager to help when called (Jeremiah 33.3).

4) Planning for you—for a hope-filled future (Jeremiah 29:11).

5) Redeeming you—all things working for good (Romans 8:28).

If your heart doesn't believe these truths, then it's time to roll up your spiritual sleeves and go to work, attaching your faith to His scriptures. Jesus said that believing the truth about God is our most important *work*.[18] Repentance is turning back to the love that never turns away from you. So, don't make Father do all the running—learn to run to Him!

The Way of Restoration

Having our hearts restored to a condition of deeply trusting our Father to never fail us or forsake us will require recognizing the moments when we begin "serving" a lesser image of God: Feeling unworthy, anxious or driven to perform are clues we need to heed.

1) Pray for the Holy Spirit to open your eyes to see any distorted images of the Father that you may be carrying: Forgive the ones who planted them; repent, renounce those fallen images.

2) Pray for Jesus to more fully reveal the Father to you: Repent, renounce all unbelief; confess the truth of His perfect love, abundant mercy, saving help, great plans and total redemption.

3) Turn to the Father and release gratitude for His never-ending love and grace-based way of saving You!

Father, I confess that I have let the enemy and my own life experiences build up false images about You that have kept me from running to You. But those days are ending now! From now on I will fight to believe in the truth about You that Jesus is revealing to me. I will fight to run to You when I am tempted or in need. I will seek Your grace even in my places of deepest disgrace. Let Your perfect love cast out all of my fears!

SECTION THREE:
STRONGHOLDS

For the weapons of our warfare are not of the flesh,
but mighty before God to the throwing down of strongholds,
throwing down imaginations and every high thing
that is exalted against the knowledge of God,
and bringing every thought into captivity
to the obedience of Christ.
2 Corinthians 10:4-5 WEB

CHAPTER 11

STRONGHOLDS

This is the real "battlefield" of the course where we will explore the major emotional strongholds that disconnect us from the peace of Christ and all too often hold us captive to stress (as anxiety) or distress (as depression). The strongholds we will explore are generational sin, unbelief, accusation, bitterness, trauma, rejection, self-rejection, envy, the occult, fear and addictions. That's quite a list! First, however, we will have to study what strongholds are, how they are formed and how they can be brought down.[1]

Jesus is our true stronghold—the Rock that we run to when threatened by sin or danger, our new shield of protection against the enemy's encroachments. David couldn't say enough about trusting the Lord as His Protector, Provider and Pardoner.

> **The Lord is my rock and my fortress and my deliverer, my God, my rock, in whom I take refuge, my shield, and the horn of my salvation, my stronghold.** Psalm 18:2

Strongholds of the Flesh

The enemy creates *counterfeit* strongholds in our flesh. These are un-surrendered, un-healed or un-crucified areas of the old nature or self-life. They rise up and resist the Spirit-given life. Self-protectiveness built them and maintains them, aided by the lies and temptations of the enemy. We are to resist them by pulling them down. Like David we don't need self-protection any longer—we have the Lord to protect us! His grace is all-sufficient!

> **For the weapons of our warfare are not of the flesh, but mighty before God to the throwing down of strongholds, throwing down imaginations and every high thing that is exalted against the knowledge of God, and bringing every thought into captivity to the obedience of Christ.** 2 Corinthians 10:4-5 WEB

Strongholds are habit structures of thought. The new birth gives us a new heart, but we have to change our former mental and emotional habits.[2] We do this by working with the truth and grace

God supplies.[3] Habits are thoughts or actions repeated so often over time that no conscious thought is required for them to take place. Thoughts begin as seeds but, if unchecked, can become as firmly rooted as trees.[4] Strongholds are built upon seemingly apparent truths which are actually distortions of eternal truth. Our continuing agreement with them keeps them built up, strengthening the grip upon us of the negative emotions which they engender. Stronghold thinking is "stinking thinking!"[5]

Such thinking springs up from the murky depths of the heart of our fallen nature which is "deceitful above all things and desperately wicked" according to the Lord, who alone can search it out.[6] Yes, as if the new life weren't complicated enough, we now have to deal with the reality of having "two hearts" in one believer. It is very comforting to know that the new heart we have received is entirely good.[7] Indeed, it is Christlike for it comes from Him and stays ever ready to power up the New Creation life, whenever we break free of the strongholds that entrap it.

The old heart, however, is the "stronghold maker." It draws its power from all of the deeply cherished (false) beliefs and (unchristian) coping strategies we developed along the way with the enemy's help. These become the wellspring for our negative emotions, for any emotion is merely the passionate expression of a deeply held belief. This helps explain why living the new life is so easy whenever we are free of negative emotions (it flows gracefully from our new heart) and yet so difficult whenever negative emotions hold us in their power (their power comes from our old heart's most cherished beliefs). We are literally wrestling *within* ourselves at times over which belief system to believe—the one that comes with Jesus or the one that we lived by apart from His leadership. If you are wondering which is which, then know that believing from the new heart *always* produces life and peace *in any moment*; believing out of the old heart's strongholds doesn't.

The Power of Strongholds

The stronghold is fortified by false beliefs which we are to pull down by carrying those thoughts captive to Christ, once the hidden lie has been exposed by the truth of God's Word. This requires diligence, especially in the beginning.[8] In the stronghold we encounter the self-life's negative power coming against us as feelings and as unbelieving thoughts. Be on guard if you find yourself thinking: "I feel it so strongly, it *feels* like it must be true." To counter this we need to wake up and realize that our feelings are lying to us. Never rely upon your feelings to declare the truth! In fact the more powerful the negative feeling is, the greater our belief still is in the lie that is at its core. However, not all positive feelings can be trusted either (see Negative Emotions).

A second problem arises whenever we "hear" ourselves thinking: "I just don't see how God's truth can be right about this situation." Realize that in certain situations your understanding is going to be worthless to you. His ways and His thoughts really are higher than ours.[9] We are told in Proverbs to get understanding, but not to *lean* upon it.[10] Cast down what you think you know if it keeps you from trusting, for trust is the highest wisdom. You can at least understand this: He loves you, He is not lying to you and He will never fail you. Tell *that* to your doubts and fears!

Strongholds are fortresses of thought built up within our flesh which can be used by the enemy to harass and oppress us. Generational sin patterns that left gaping holes in our covering and the unhealed wounds of traumatic events often cause strongholds to form. Usually they have been built "stone by stone" (thought by thought) over a long period of time, so long in fact that we have forgotten that we ever believed or felt anything else or that life was ever different from how the stronghold now makes it seem. In that area of experience we have come to see life from the perspective of the stronghold. Like the keep of a medieval castle it is well-fortified. We feel protected by believing it, but it "keeps" us a prisoner on the inside. We are held captive by our own walls, and these walls also keep others from leading us out. Choose to take your walls down and let others (and the truth they bring) in.

Discerning a stronghold area in your life is a necessary first step towards bringing it down. If you can't just say no to the flesh, you are dealing with a stronghold built upon that area of your fallen nature. Another way of picturing these strongholds of the flesh is like having your arm gripped by someone dragging you along with them against your will. The enemy gains a strong *hold* upon our flesh in areas where we have repeatedly given our beliefs and actions over to his twisted words and ways.

Strongholds are habit structures of thought, not evil spirits. A stronghold may be occupied or unoccupied—this is by no means easy to discern. Try to attack someone else's stronghold head on and it may seem well-occupied and well-defended against all the reasons you bring. This *may* be an indication of the enemy's direct involvement. Likewise, if a spirit is oppressing you *through* a stronghold of your own, you may sense the power of the negative feelings it stirs up and the tenacious hold those thoughts and feelings have over you. Evil spirits are very stubborn, not easily giving way to truth and to the exercise of our wills to resist them. Fortunately, it is not necessary to know if a spirit is oppressing you. Let the Holy Spirit show you what sins to confess and what false beliefs to renounce, then choose to submit to God and His truth. Genuine submission to God undercuts the evil spirit's right to remain, and determined rebuking makes them flee.[11]

Strongholds take advantage of the enemy's great lie that you can never really feel good about yourself or be at peace within yourself unless everything is going your way and the people you care about are all affirming you. What a formula for disaster that is! Stemming from this kind of thinking we may find ourselves living under an inner demand to a) never goof up, b) never get rejected and c) always be capable of solving problems (a) and (b) if they do occur. Protestant Reformers called this "works righteousness"—tying to advance our cause by our own works. We call it perfectionism and performance orientation. Either way it's a snare of the enemy. The truth is that you can feel incredibly good about yourself whenever you choose by a living faith to get your eyes off yourself and back on to the One who remains steadfast at loving you and patiently leads you step-by-step whenever you trust Him enough to do it.

Pulling Down Strongholds

How are strongholds brought down? The things that bring strongholds down are the very things that would have kept them from forming in the first place—having sufficient understanding of how to apply the truth of God's Word to the hurtful situation or wrong desire. So now in the present moment when new situations trigger the stronghold, we can do what we didn't do then and begin taking the stronghold down one victory at a time, under the Spirit's power. We do this by carrying their "high" thoughts captive to Christ.[12] This is primarily a truth encounter on our part. We choose by an act of our will to cast down our understanding and break agreement with our feelings. As we agree with the truth (that the enemy's stronghold is a lie and God's Word is the truth), then the Holy Spirit strengthens and raises us. Confessing truth and renouncing the lies need to be done by the one seeking freedom—thought by thought, "stone by stone."

Either we will carry wrong thoughts captive to Christ, or those wrong thoughts will carry us captive to do their will.[13] Therefore, there is a great need to pray for revelation because if we lack discernment the un-recognized thoughts have greater power.[14] Recognizing stronghold thinking and being willing to challenge it with the truths of God's Word, gives us the weapons needed for victory. Truth is always liberating—if you truly believe it.

> **So Jesus said to the Jews who had believed in him, "If you abide in my word, you are truly my disciples, and you will know the truth, and the truth will set you free."** John 8:31-32

Basic discipleship and inner healing dismantle strongholds. Basic discipleship is the part we play by doing our best with the faith and self-discipline that we have available to us. Disciplines act as a restraint upon the power of temptation and of our fallen nature and its strongholds. If you think that restraining your flesh isn't working, just imagine abandoning the discipline or the faith you still have left to you and "see" how disastrous that would likely become. In the grip of a very trying time, we usually can't see how to make things better, but we certainly can make them worse! What are the disciplines? Regular prayer, Bible study, worship, fellowship and service to others combined with seeking to trust and obey the Lord form the backbone of basic discipleship.

Basic discipleship enables us to prune unwanted fruit off our spiritual tree; inner healing gets at the root issues that caused strongholds to form bad fruit in the first place. Where there is bad fruit, there is almost always a root issue to deal with.[15] Inner healing removes or breaks the power of temptations and of our fallen nature by bringing release from the pain and/or ungodly beliefs trapped inside due to past traumatic events (see Chapter 16). Now that we understand the need for "pruning shears" and "garden spades" we are ready to explore specific stronghold areas in each of the chapters that follow.

The Way to Freedom

There is an underlying pattern to finding freedom from the negative emotion strongholds. It is the way of "returning and rest," of repentance and restoration by entrusting the whole of our life to God, especially in the area of our present trouble.[16]

1) The first step to freedom from any stronghold is realizing that you have lost the peace of Christ, are being held captive instead by a negative emotion, and that this is a spiritual problem.

2) The next step is to take full responsibility for agreeing with the enemy in that area which the stronghold represents: Repent, renounce and carry it captive to Christ until you see something in Him that restores your trust in God and willingness to obey.

3) Turn to the Father and release gratitude to Him for the mercy, love, power and promises He showers upon you by His grace!

Father, I have lived inside the walls of my strongholds for so long they have become a part of me, but I do want to find out what life in Your Kingdom is like on the other side of these walls. Lead me in the way of childlike trust and simplicity of heart! I ask you to help me take all of my strongholds down, untruth by untruth, and rebuild with Your truths the godly walls of love and mercy, faith and grace around the renewed heart You are giving me through Jesus. What I can't tear down, will You? Come charge my walls! Send, allow, withhold—do whatever it takes so that our two hearts can meet and beat as one in this life.

CHAPTER 12

REVERSING THE CURSE

The Stronghold of Generational Sin

While still in the womb, without any initiation or cooperation on our part, the devastating consequence of Adam's sin was imparted to us: We were all born with a sin nature separating us from God. This is the deep wellspring of all the generational sins against us which followed and it will not be removed in our lifetime, unless the Lord returns first. Fortunately, we can become free of the impact of ancestral sins in our generational line by reducing or eliminating their "strong hold" upon us.

As it happens, the first unavoidable strongholds any of us encounter are not our own, though they may very well become our own. They are the strongholds of generational patterns of sin in families. Before we were conceived these strongholds were already in place. Since no one is perfect, every family line has sin patterns which negatively influence succeeding generations. We can see the evidence of this: Children of alcoholics often become alcoholics, many diseases run in families and some children are born with dreadful genetic defects. Life is tough enough, so it hardly seems fair that the sins of previous generations could be allowed by God to have *any* impact, let alone a devastating impact at times, on the lives of innocent newborns. The question has to be asked: How can it be right for children to be "punished" for the sins of their ancestors? Why do we suffer from sins in the past?

Why the Problem Exists

The important thing to keep in mind is that because God lives outside of time, un-repented sin is always a fresh stain before the eyes of the Lord: He sees past wrongs as *present* sins. This is why generational sin continues to "live on" even after the person who sinned has died—that sin was their choice and God sustains the reality of the world formed by our choosing. This is the dignity and the terrible responsibility of being given free will in a real world.

Upholding the "moral order" we choose to create is part of God's self-revelation to Moses: The sin ledger isn't canceled at death.

> **The Lord passed before him and proclaimed, "The Lord... a God merciful and gracious... but who will by no means clear the guilty, visiting the iniquity of the fathers on the children and the children's children, to the third and the fourth generation."** Exodus 34:6-7

Un-repented sin doesn't just evaporate; it continues to wreak havoc in the generations. Since the time of Abel the blood still cries out from the ground.[1] Lest we get the wrong idea, God is not the one doing the punishing—He punished Jesus for our sins fully and completely. God does not willingly desire to see us afflicted.[2] It is the reality of choice that He gives to "the fathers" that releases the consequences of their iniquities on the earth. By choosing sin, we "choose" the consequences of sin to come, even to the following generations. God has "no choice" but to allow the "punishing" effects of sin to visit the earth until someone recognizes it as sin, takes responsibility and carries it captive to Him. We may rightly cherish our heritage (generational blessing is very real), but we need to also be honest about the sinful side and bring it to God. This kind of responsible repentance is what God desires.[3]

> **"But if they confess their iniquity and the iniquity of their fathers... and they make amends for their iniquity, then I will remember my covenant with Jacob."** Leviticus 26:40-42

The Pattern Is Not Compulsory

No one has to walk in the sins of their fathers (or mothers). The reality of sin's effects on the generations does not mean that children have no free will, but that un-repented sin creates a negative legacy within the family and the nation. For good or ill, whether intended or not, "like begets like" by an invariable mandate of the original creative process.[4] In Ezekiel the Lord speaks of each individual's responsibility for their sin and the ultimate penalty (death). The son will not die as a direct result of the father's sins; each person stands (or falls) as an individual.

> **"The soul who sins shall die... Now suppose this man fathers a son who sees all the sins that his father has done; he sees, and does not**

do likewise... he shall not die for his father's iniquity; he shall surely live." Ezekiel 18:4, 14, 17

Although, the righteous avoidance of the father's sins is a shield against the curse, *only repentance* can remove sin and its effects (past or present). Remember that God as a responsible Creator has to maintain true justice and therefore He "by no means clears the guilty."[5] He can only put sin and its consequences under the Blood of Christ if one of us repents and asks for mercy. Until then we, who still hold dominion over the earth, are choosing (often unknowingly) to let the curse of past misdeeds remain in effect. Let us also keep in mind that God's stated desire is to pass on blessings. Surely He chooses our parents to pass on the blessings of their generations—not the curses.

"Visiting the iniquity of the fathers on the children... but showing steadfast love to thousands of those who love me and keep my commandments." Exodus 20:5-6

How the Patterns Get Passed Down

We were "programmed" by the enemy from birth—set up by sin in the generations going all the way back to the Garden. God makes us "very good" in the womb,[6] but even as He is working to create us in His Image, the sin of Adam and the sins of our fathers were also at work, "unmaking" us into something less than God intended. The enemy was working against us before we were born, hating us "without cause."[7] If we fail to understand this reality, we will unwittingly blame God by "crediting" Him for fallen ways that we and others may have: "I hate being shy (or hot tempered or nervous, etc.), but that's just the way God made me!" No it isn't, that's the way the enemy bent and bruised you by sinning against you in ways that you couldn't notice or can't recall. Our personality structure according to psychologists is shaped in early childhood.[8] How much of that shaping process do you remember? Consider these two powerful personality shapers that are not of God:

1) Adam's sin has blocked all of his children from being born as God intended—united to His love and living in His Presence.

85

2) The sins of preceding generations as they reached us through our bloodline, through the womb, and through our home environment began to set root issues and carnal patterns in us.[9]

There are three ways that the curse (sin's consequences) may be passed down the generations:[10]

1) Nature: Our genetic inheritance can be physiological and psychological. Damage in the genetic code at birth does not come from God's design or intervention, but results from the effects of the Fall upon humanity. God's work is without defect.

2) Nurture: The emotional environment and training in the home shapes each child. The good that is in us often passes into our children (we like that!), but so does the bad.

3) Spiritual: Spirits drawn to families (due to habitual sins) may carry patterns of the curse down the family line.[11]

Evidence for Generational Patterns

It doesn't require faith in God or the Bible to see evidence of generational patterns. For instance, doctors routinely take family histories because many diseases are known to run in families. As with prayer or anything else God does, we cannot exactly describe how He works or prove spiritual realities against all doubt. Nevertheless, consider the following story as further uncanny evidence for the truth of both generational sin and blessing.

A study was done in the eighteenth century of the lives of two men.[12] One of them, Max Jukes, lived in New York in the late 1700s. He did not seem to believe in Christ or pursue a Christian manner of life. He had 709 known descendants. These included 280 pauperized adults and 140 criminals: 7 murderers, 128 prostitutes, 280 described as harlots and 60 who became thieves. His family members cost the state $1,308,000 (a staggering sum in those days)—and they made few positive contributions to society.

Jonathan Edwards lived in the same state at the same time. He loved and served the Lord, raising his children in church. Of his 1394 descendants there were "practically no lawbreakers": by actual count, more than 100 lawyers, 30 judges, 13 college presidents, 100 professors, 60 authors, 60 doctors, 100 ministers and missionaries, 75 military officers, and 80 elected to public office. His family never burdened the state, but contributed immeasurably to the common good. You cannot change your ancestors, but you can significantly impact the generations that follow you.

The Motivational Power of This Truth

This lesson on the consequences of generational sin is not meant to put anyone on a fear trip (about what sins may lie with their ancestors) or a guilt trip (about what they may be passing on to their children). Let it be a *reality* trip. The fact is that our lives powerfully impact other people—especially our natural or spiritual children—whether we want them to or not. It is important to know this because one of the enemy's favorite tactics is discouragement when we are down: "No one cares about you…your life doesn't matter to anyone." That's a lie! All of heaven cares about you and stands ready to pass on your every effort to be faithful as a benefit to someone else down the line. There is at least an echo of this reality in the psalmist's choice to make his stand for truth be something that would powerfully affect *all* later generations. And do you know something? It has! God preserved that psalmist's witness and it continues to uplift us even to this day.

> **I will sing of the steadfast love of the Lord, forever; with my mouth I will make known your faithfulness to all generations.** Psalm 89:1

The knowledge of this truth can be a powerful weapon in our arsenal against the enemy. Let it spur you on to heroic efforts of hanging in there when the going gets tough, because your life really matters! Desperate or discouraging moments may come when we are going to need motivations larger than ourselves to keep our feet moving in the right direction. The truth is that living for oneself alone is not sufficient motivation for anyone. It was never meant to be. If we are only seeking our own comfort, or success, or satisfaction, then those self-centered motivations will often fail us in the times of trial. We will need to learn to reach for better, stronger and higher motives if we want to find the inner strength to keep from quitting when the chips are down.

God supplies that strength whenever we realize that the lives of people we love hang in the balance. It matters to your children that you are trying to be faithful—even if they don't know it, even if it is killing you, even if it doesn't seem to be making any difference in your eyes. It even matters to the generations that haven't been born yet. And in addition to natural children, God also supplies those in our lives who are a spiritual heritage. Like Paul we are all raising the next generation.[13] Will it be for good or for ill? You decide!

"But as for me and my house, we will serve the Lord." Joshua 24:15

The Way to Freedom

Many generational patterns of sin are hard to recognize because it seems like that's just the way things are: "Doesn't everyone act that way?" Other patterns are hard to escape because from an early age we resented family members for sinning against us and those bitter judgments bound us to their behaviors.

1) Once you discern that a family pattern is not of God, be sure that you fully forgive the family members who are caught in it.

2) Then take full responsibility for agreeing with it and walking in it yourself: Repent, renounce and carry it captive to Christ until you can release it to Him for His help in removing it.

3) Turn to the Father and release gratitude to Him that He is working to overturn every curse with a greater good!

Dear Heavenly Father, in the Name of Jesus, I choose by an act of my will to forgive my father (or other family member) for all the ways that he failed me or hurt me. I renounce the sins in my generational line and I repent for having walked in them myself. Forgive me and break their power over me. I put the Blood of Jesus between me and any generational sin and I cancel all assignments of the enemy in Jesus' Name. I choose to fully accept myself as the child of the father You gave me. Holy Spirit please come... heal my broken heart and show me and tell me Your Truth.

CHAPTER 13

THE POWER OF BELIEVING

The Stronghold of Unbelief

Due to Adam's sin, we were all born into a condition of not knowing our God. Unbelief, therefore, is the primary obstacle that every person on earth needs to overcome, since the faith connection to God has to be restored in order for us to be saved by His grace.[1] Surprisingly, unbelief continues to be the primary obstacle that believers need to overcome. But wait! Wouldn't it make more sense to say this of un-believers? Certainly, unbelief is a huge obstacle for them—they're still spiritually blind from birth—but that doesn't diminish its power and effectiveness against those of us whose eyes have been opened by faith. In fact it is often (if not always) the thing that we don't see which trips us up. All Christians will tell you that they believe in Jesus. But have we been "blinded" by the light? The all-important issue of believing doesn't end there. The demons also believe that the Father and Jesus exist, but *they take no joy or peace in believing it,* nor do they live yielded to Him in trust and obedience.[2]

Since we are saved by grace *through faith,* it is entirely by means of faith that we are meant to access all that grace so freely supplies.[3] For instance, God's Word says that we who *believe* can be filled with all joy and peace "in believing."[4] If this is not what you are experiencing *all day long,* then perhaps there are a few things you still need to learn about recognizing and overcoming the stronghold of unbelief which may be quenching your faith.

The Active Power of New Life

Believing is the active power of the new life—the power that activates the life that God desires to give us by His grace. The critical issue is believing God's written Word with a *full* heart of faith. John says that he wrote his gospel in order for us to believe and to find life *by believing* (review Chapter 8).

But these are written so that you may believe that Jesus is the Christ, the Son of God, and that by believing you may have life in his name. John 20:31

What John means by life is more than mere existence and it is not limited to heaven only. John is writing about a quality of life that is filled with joy, peace and love—what the Bible calls eternal life, New Creation life, or abundant life. Peter says that *through believing* we can find joy in the midst of trials and even receive the "end" or goal of our faith, the "salvation" of our souls—that is, experience peace and confidence of heart and mind *in this life*.

> **In this you rejoice, though now for a little while, if necessary, you have been grieved by various trials... Though you do not now see him, you believe in him and rejoice with joy that is inexpressible and filled with glory, obtaining the outcome of your faith, the salvation of your souls.** 1 Peter 1:6, 8-9

There is evidently a way to hold our faith, even in the midst of hard trials, so that we have inexpressible and glorious joy—deep, inward encouragement. This is not will power. You cannot fake this kind of joy or work it up by your own efforts. This joy is something anyone can experience by learning to fully believe God's truth *in the midst of a trial*. But not just any truth will do! The feeling of being tried in our faith comes directly from a lack of trust in God about the situation. Therefore, being united by faith to the *right* truth about God will automatically begin producing joy in you as your trust is restored.[5] That is the power of the Holy Spirit. Such joy is the fruit of dealing with unbelief and learning to activate faith with the truth of God's Word.[6] But know this: Very often your feelings, your understanding and your circumstances will seem to be shouting out that God's Word can't be true for you.

Unbelief is a stronghold that the enemy has built into every believer. We all have limits to what we are presently able to believe *about* God ("Does He love me *in this*?") and to what we are able to believe God *for* ("Will He help me *with this*?"). If this were not so we would already be filled with the joy that Peter says can be ours in the midst of our trials—just as Paul and Silas experienced in prison.[7] If we are not there yet, it is vital that we begin to learn to recognize the ways in which our own unbelief is limiting our growth in the Lord and keeping us bound to patterns of the past. Unbelief is also a block to healing. Jesus could not do many healings in Nazareth because of the town's spiritual climate of unbelief.[8] The lack of miraculous healings and supernatural events in the Western church may be a warning sign that a climate of unbelief surrounds us also.

Believing God at His Word

Biblical faith in God is fully believing God at His Word, even in the face of great adversity. Such faith believes that God is true to His Word.[9] Unbelief is the opposite of faith in God and His Word. Unbelief is the sin of hardness of heart that doesn't trust God's Person, purposes or promises. Unbelief is the stronghold that kept God's people out of the land promised to them as their inheritance.

> **Therefore, as the Holy Spirit says, "Today, if you hear his voice, do not harden your hearts as in the rebellion… As I swore in my wrath, 'They shall not enter my rest.'" Take care, brothers, lest there be in any of you an evil, unbelieving heart, leading you to fall away from the living God.** Hebrews 3:7-8, 11-12

Forty years of wandering in the wilderness happened to the children of Israel because they drew back in fear and unbelief from following God and Moses into the Promised Land, their place of "rest." Have you been wandering, seeking rest, yet finding none? Our promised place of rest is "the peace of God, which surpasses all understanding"—the peace that Jesus gives us in any situation whenever we surrender our fears and our obedience to Him and abide in Him.[10] *There is no peace without complete surrender.* There is no abiding in rest without being willing to trust and obey.[11] Sometimes we have to labor to enter that rest.[12] Always we have to keep watch lest the enemy "draw us away" from our new life of trust and obedience.[13] Our promised land is a life of abundant joy and peace lived in close relationship with Jesus Christ in this life and the next. Although heaven is promised to all who believe, God's Kingdom on earth is promised to those who engage the battle of fighting to exercise their faith.

91

From the days of John the Baptist until now the kingdom of heaven has suffered violence, and the violent take it by force. Matthew 11:12

A convincing temptation to doubt God's Word precipitated the Fall into sin. So convincing is the enemy's deception, that at critical points in our growth we will find it much easier to believe the lies that the enemy has sown into our lives, than the truths from God's Word that the Holy Spirit is seeking to teach us. Forewarned is forearmed! Let us never forget that the Word of the Lord is the effective instrument by which everything that now exists was created. All of creation is a testimony to the truth and power of God's Word to create and to sustain life.[14] It is impossible that God could ever speak forth a Word that would not be true—His Word is truth.[15] He cannot lie.[16] Yet, there is one whose word should never be trusted. From the beginning God's Word has been contested by Satan. He seeks to "father" us into believing his lies, seeing from his distorted perspective and walking in his false ways.

You are of your father the devil, and your will is to do your father's desires. He was a murderer from the beginning, and has nothing to do with the truth, because there is no truth in him. When he lies, he speaks out of his own character, for he is a liar and the father of lies. John 8:44

God seeks a people who will serve Him in Spirit and truth.[17] God's answer to the Fall was to cultivate a son of Adam who would believe God at His Word and therefore become the spiritual father to a nation of restored believers. In calling Abraham, God promised him great things which Abraham at first gladly believed.[18] Notice, however, that God did not make it easy for Abraham to go on believing the promises. The unexpectedly long delay between the promises and their fulfillment (with the birth of Isaac) severely tested Abraham's ability to believe God's Word. Just like Abraham, we too have been given magnificent, life-giving promises through God's Word. Some of these promises have to do with who He is to us; some have to do with who we are in Him; some have to do with what our life in God could become. Just as it was with Abraham, God's delays may make it hard to believe His promises. Sometimes they may seem impossible to believe at all.

We may stagger in unbelief, but we must learn Abraham's way, who, "contrary to hope, in hope believed," if we are to reap the full life of faith offered to us and enter our Promised Land.[19]

By which he has granted to us his precious and very great promises, so that through them you may become partakers of the divine nature. 2 Peter 1:4

Unbelief Is Believing in Un-truth

There are two formidable challenges to everyone's faith: our own understanding and our feelings. We are not to lean on our understanding or be led by our feelings.[20] Trusting in God with our whole heart means the quality of our new life will depend upon our ability to find joy and peace *through our faith in God* even when our understanding can't understand and our feelings are kicking and screaming. That kind of believing in God is hard work at times, but this is the real work we are called to do.

Jesus answered them, "This is the work of God, that you believe in him whom he has sent." John 6:29

It was unbelief in the truth of God's Word that broke the world God created. Believing in untruth has been breaking hearts and breaking down lives ever since. Watch out for these deceptive, deadly "Ds": doubt, discouragement, despair and depression— they are all rooted in *active unbelief*, even if surrounded by *passive faith*. Jesus has come that we might know the truth. And by the truths He shows us and by the faith He gives us, we would be made free. However, for His truths to work for us, we often have to work very hard at believing them and become adept at casting down *all* unbelief. Even a tiny bit of unbelief can be sufficient to block the faith we are seeking to exercise from liberating our heart. However, fully believing the truth will *automatically* restore peace, joy, confidence in God and bright hope into our hearts.

So Jesus said to the Jews who had believed in him, "If you abide in my word, you are truly my disciples, and you will know the truth, and the truth will set you free." John 8:31-32

Fortunately, we do not have to work at believing in God and His Word by will power and good intentions. No stronghold can be defeated in our own strength. God is gracious and willing to help us with our areas of unbelief. Be bold in confessing your distrust as the sin it is. Don't be afraid to admit to God how often unbelief may be ruling over you. He sees it clearly and loves you anyway! Unbelief in God's Word can block healing, keep us from receiving the blessings of God and prevent us from entering the Kingdom on earth, but it cannot separate us from His love.[21] No one prayer can guarantee humility or ultimate victory, but the distraught father's prayer for his son's deliverance is a good beginning, "Lord, I believe; help [me overcome] my unbelief!"[22]

The Way to Freedom

The most difficult thing about getting free of unbelief is recognizing that it is working *on* you, since it feels so natural and seems like such a reasonable reaction given the circumstances. But we are called to the higher life of an active faith based on what is "unfelt" and unseen—the rock-solid promises of our God!

1) Be ready to pounce on any deflating or despairing thought, realizing that any loss of bright hope or confidence is not coming from your true self, but from a spirit of unbelief.

2) Take full responsibility for agreeing with it: Repent, renounce and carry it captive to Christ until you see something in Him that restores your trust and confidence in God.

3) Turn to the Father and release gratitude to Him that He loves and accepts you even when your faith is riddled with unbelief!

Father, it is not my faith that saves me—I am being saved by Your love, Your truth, Jesus' Blood, and the Holy Spirit's power. Forgive me for taking credit for what I believe (for You alone opened my eyes) and for turning a blind eye to what I have not been believing (that You have already shown me to be true). I cast down all past pride and fear. I want to become able to see this hidden stronghold when it is blocking me. Help me to believe what You believe.

CHAPTER 14

DISCERNING THE ENEMY

The Stronghold of Accusation

If the Lord were the only "outsider" dropping thoughts into us, our lives would be so much simpler, but there is another kingdom speaking to us, seeking to bring us into agreement with its ways of thinking and acting upon the earth. One of the strategies of that other kingdom is to make its thoughts seem like our own thoughts or God's thoughts—so that wrong thoughts will go unrecognized. Therefore, there is a great need on our part to learn to *discern* these hidden ways of the enemy and to *recognize* his voice (the fourth Kingdom key). This stronghold of accusation comes early in this sequence of lessons on strongholds because the voice of the Accuser came on the scene early in the Garden and early in our own lives as well. Be on guard! To the one being deceived the condemning thoughts never seem like accusations suggested by an invisible enemy: They always seem like truth-telling about God, self or others coming from our own reasoning process.

Paul said that the Early Church was no longer "ignorant of his devices" concerning the enemy and his ways.[1] We need to make sure those same lights have been turned on for us! For instance, the "voice" of the Accuser has both a content of accusing words and an oppressive tone in the way those thoughts are formed—a nagging pressure beating down, but never building up. The Holy Spirit doesn't speak that way. The writer of Hebrews says that our discernment grows as our "senses," not just our minds, are trained by "reason of use."[2] Let your spiritual senses, as well as your intellect, become fine-tuned at recognizing the difference. This can only come with time and the Holy Spirit's help, but don't worry, you are certain to have plenty of opportunities for practice!

Accusation Separates and Condemns

Many incurable sicknesses are rooted in the areas of separation that accusation produces between God, self and others. Such "stress fractures" break down the body's health over time just as their physical counterparts do material structures in the natural world. Accusation is also a block to healing because it invariably leads to bitterness which blocks both healing and answered prayer.[3] Speaking in a condemning way against the Lord's anointed servants also brings severe consequences.[4] Scratch the surface and you will likely find that accusations lie behind all of the deeply implanted false beliefs which cause mental illness, addictions and stress related diseases. Clearly, this is a major realm of the enemy's operations.

Satan and his kingdom deceive, tempt, destroy *and accuse*. Every time the enemy seeks to tempt us into agreement with his ways by deceptive thoughts, he is also seeking to divide us from our sources of life and strength, and by so doing, destroy us. Accusation is dangerous precisely because it is so divisive—it is the enemy coming between us and God. Accusations isolate us by separating us from others and by drawing us away from the peace of Christ.[5] The fruit of accusation can include doubt, confusion, turmoil, fear, suspicion, jealousy, bitter judgment, and a whole lot more. The Accuser divides by using *truth with a twist* in ways that are hard to recognize and seem very convincing. He works to separate us:

1) From God, His Word or His Person[6]

2) From our true self, as God see us[7]

3) From others, as God sees them[8]

Accusation and condemnation are the exact opposite of what God is doing through Christ. Paul says that God neither accuses, nor condemns us.[9] His desire is for the one in sin to be gently restored.[10] Until death comes, there is always hope for restoration to God and separation from sins through repentance, grace and faith. We are meant to keep Jesus' hard won victory and heaven's hope-filled perspective in our hearts *towards everyone*. So let's settle this once and for all: Accusation and condemnation come from the enemy—not God. Satan measures out his criticisms and charges with just enough apparent truth to hook us—but he always twists our thoughts away from God's perspective of love and mercy. His activity is described as unrelenting and unceasing.[11] "Radio Satan" is always "on the air." We have to learn to detect it and change channels.

From Genesis to Revelation

Let's review how accusation got its start. Satan, whose name means "Adversary," began with accusations against God's Word in the Garden.[12] Adam and Eve were drawn away from trusting God and fell into separation from God and spiritual death along with it. Although they did not realize it, they now had a new father—the devil—whose nature entered them and whose own image and ways were beginning to distort the Image of God they carried.[13] When the Lord returned to find them, He said something astonishing to Adam: "Who told you that you were naked?"[14] God's question to Adam was meant to open his eyes to see that the Accuser was still speaking to him, no longer through the snake, but through Adam's own thought processes.[15] Under the pressure of inward condemnation, Adam accused Eve of being the reason he chose to sin. His words also carried a veiled accusation against God for giving Eve to him in the first place. Then Eve joined in by accusing the serpent, thus trying to shift blame from herself to the source of her temptation. By one fell swoop the Accuser succeeded in subverting humanity to do his work of accusation for him and they were *completely unaware of his instigations!*[16]

Now zoom forward to see how accusation went global. Having established his kingdom through such slight devices of accusation in the Garden, the enemy handily expanded his operations to cover the earth. John on Patmos was given a vision of the Accuser as no longer being a lowly serpent, but a mighty dragon.

> **And the great dragon was thrown down, that ancient serpent, who is called the devil and Satan, the deceiver of the whole world—he was thrown down to the earth, and his angels were thrown down with him. And I heard a loud voice in heaven, saying, "Now the salvation and the power and the kingdom of our God and the authority of his Christ have come, for the accuser of our brothers has been thrown down, who accuses them day and night before our God.**
> Revelation 12:9-10

Notice that salvation, strength, Kingdom and power come when this formidable enemy is cast down. The choice is before us: Will we serve the Accuser or will we make a quality decision to cast down all accusations that try to rise up within us against God, self or others? Let the voice from the Garden become silenced. Turn off "radio Satan" and live in the Kingdom!

Recognize Accusing Thoughts

Accusation is a counterfeit of the true knowledge of God, a wrong use of genuine discernment. The Holy Spirit may indeed allow us to see sin in another person or one's self, but a spirit of accusation will seek to turn it into bitter judgments that bind the person to their sin and separate us from them. Learn to recognize the voice of the Accuser—the way self-condemnation speaks *to you* or the way offended self-righteousness seeks to speak *through you* to others. We are indeed called to discern good and evil, but one of the greatest evils is to accuse or judge another.[17] Seek to be aware of where your thoughts are coming from. Check the source! Godly thoughts come from God's Word, other people (speaking by the Spirit), the Holy Spirit and our renewed mind. Accusing thoughts come from the world, other people (speaking by the enemy), an accusing spirit or our un-renewed mind.

We are meant to cast down "every high thing that exalts itself" against God.[18] Accusation is a "high thing" because it elevates us above others in judgment of them and because it "exalts itself" within us against God's direct command to stop doing it. Learn to discern and cast down even your unvoiced accusations against God (anger, unbelief, discouragement); against others (judgments, un-forgiveness, slander); and against self (condemnation, shame, regret). Instead, join with Jesus in continual intercession.[19] There is always room for one more on the Mercy Seat!

Discerning between conviction versus condemnation is also key to living a life of grace, since so much that we most immediately experience of sin is its indwelling presence with us. We don't want to live in denial, blind to our own faults nor do we want to live burdened by guilt and feelings of self-reproach, blind to the grace of God. How can you tell the difference between conviction by the Holy Spirit versus condemnation by the enemy? It takes a lot of trial and error, but here are a few guidelines. Conviction shows us the problem and offers a way out; condemnation makes us the problem and seals the exits. Conviction is a gentle voice embracing us with quiet acceptance; condemnation breathes out threats of judgment and displeasure. Under conviction we may feel sorrow for those we have hurt; under condemnation we feel sorry for ourselves. Conviction leads to life; condemnation leads to death. The difference is dramatic, though often difficult to discern under the pressure of events. Don't give up and you'll get it!

> **I now rejoice, not that you were made sorry, but that you were made sorry to repentance. For you were made sorry in a godly way... For godly sorrow works repentance to salvation, which brings no regret. But the sorrow of the world works death.** 2 Corinthians 7:9-11 WEB

Conviction by the Spirit	Condemnation by the enemy
Always points to true guilt	Often heaps on false guilt
Knows grace exists	No grace exists
Contrition (sorry you sinned)	Feeling worthless (sorry sinner)
Targets your sin (*that was wrong*)	Attacks your person (*you're bad*)
Explains, reasons, corrects	Accuses, condemns, reprimands
Illuminates your path	Darkens your understanding
Specific wrong is clarified	Fog of general wrongness
Brings repentance	Spreads confusion
Feels light and right	Feels heavy and wrong
May not be ready to repent, but you agree with truth.	Will to confess to anything, but you still can't get free.

Let's look at it this way: Repenting of true sins brings restoration and freedom from true guilt. Confess the sin (this requires faith in Christ's shed Blood) *and receive God's mercy.* On the other hand, resisting the accusations of the enemy produces freedom from condemnation. Confess the truth (this requires courage to live what you believe about your right standing with God through Christ) *and resist the devil.* See the difference? That's discernment!

If you are still in need of freedom, reconnect quickly and powerfully by taking the Hebrews 4:16 "elevator" to the top: Go boldly to the throne of grace, get the mercy you need to reestablish your heart, get grace to help you believe in the mercy, then stand against the Accuser.

Let us then with confidence draw near to the throne of grace, that we may receive mercy and find grace to help in time of need.
Hebrews 4:16

The Way to Freedom

Little progress can be made until godly discernment comes so prayer may be needed to recognize judgmental thoughts as being wrong! Also, because we reap what we sow, our accusations aimed against others will hinder our progress at becoming free from the pain of their accusations against us and of our own inward self-condemning thoughts. We must become committed to mercy—all the way around.[20]

1) As you recognize your own accusing or condemning thoughts against others: Repent, renounce and carry those thoughts captive to Christ, interceding for them instead.

2) As you recognize the pain of accusations against you by others: Forgive them, carrying those thoughts and feelings captive to Christ until your focus on *His* love for you is restored.

3) As soon as you sense condemnation or feelings of unworthiness weighing you down: Go boldly to the throne of grace to receive the Father's mercy, then rebuke the Accuser!

Father, help me truly repent of all the accusing thoughts I have cherished towards others and all of the hurtful accusing words I have spoken. Forgive me and break the power of what I have done in agreement with the Accuser and help all those get free of any pain I have caused. Grant that I would become an intercessor for, not an accuser of others. As I become more of a grace-giver who shows mercy to others, may Your mercy capture my heart even where my own sins and sinfulness are concerned. Teach me how to "look up" and let even my failings springboard me into greater joy in the saving love that is streaming to me from Your throne of grace.

CHAPTER 15

FREEDOM THROUGH FORGIVING

The Stronghold of Bitterness

In the previous chapter we exposed the "hidden" work of the enemy to divide us from God, others and even from ourselves—by accusations that turn us from God's way of mercy-giving love. Accusations seek to create division and separation over issues of hurt and offense and then hold it all in place by means of un-forgiveness. So what is God's answer? *Forgive!* How much, how often, how thoroughly? As much as needed, as often as needed, as thoroughly as needed—to fully release your heart. The truth is a childlike heart of joy is waiting for all of us on the other side of fully forgiving the very ones who the enemy used to rob us of our joy. God really wants to turn the tables on the enemy, but He needs us to work with Him, not against Him. *Un-forgiveness in all of its forms is an agreement with Satan, not God.* It not only hardens our hearts (separating us from peace and joy), but it also damages our bodies (through the stress response). These strongholds have to be torn down if we ever want to live a grace-filled life and become champion grace givers like our glorious Lord!

Bitterness Is Not Your Friend

Bitterness holds in place a host of deadly emotions. Many people have testified that being bitter is like drinking poison and hoping the other person will die. Thanks to modern medical science we now know that grudges really do terrible things to our bodies, as well as to our relationships. Choose to get well rather than to get even. The writer of Hebrews warns that if we have a root of bitterness it will trouble us and defile many others through their contact with us.

> **Strive for peace with everyone, and for the holiness without which no one will see the Lord. See to it that no one fails to obtain the grace of God; that no "root of bitterness" springs up and causes trouble, and by it many become defiled.** Hebrews 12:14-15

Bitterness is a very damaging stressor to the body, directly leading to illness. However, unforgiveness also keeps trauma from being healed and that adversely affects our health as well. Un-mended trauma of the past always increases the levels of anxiety and fear we carry which, like bitterness, are very harmful to health. The pain of an unforgiven offense is "warning" us that God and others can't be trusted, keeping us "on guard" and fear-filled. Bitterness is also a block to healing because God has written that He will not release the extra measures of mercy we need or answer prayer if we don't show mercy.[1]

> **Whenever you stand praying, forgive, if you have anything against anyone; so that your Father, who is in heaven, may also forgive you your transgressions. But if you do not forgive, neither will your Father in heaven forgive your transgressions.** Mark 11:25-26 WEB

Bitterness is not your friend. Learn to carry it captive before it carries you captive.[2] The high thought of bitterness is saying to God, "My law of not forgiving is better than Your law of mercy."[3] Fall completely out of agreement with its thoughts and feelings, before what begins as a seed of hurt or offense grows into a stronghold of nightmarish proportions. Bitterness never stays where you put it, rather it seeks to grow and spread. It wants to take over your life. There are at least seven stages of bitterness, an ascending order of descent into darkness: un-forgiveness (not letting go of hurt), resentment ("re-feeling" old offenses; keeping a record of wrongs), retaliation (getting even by criticism, passive aggressive behavior), anger and wrath (sudden upsurge toward the other person or down upon oneself), hatred (detesting, despising, strong disliking, hardness, apathy), violence (wanting to see harm come to another), and murder (with the tongue, or in the heart, or by criminal act; wishing them dead).[4]

Resisting the Stronghold

There is massive power released when forgiveness is combined with actively believing God's promises of redemption. Forgiving others truly releases the pain and weight of wrong off of us, but we may still feel saddened by the loss we experienced. To help us recover a rightful sense of fullness, God has given magnificent promises of the restoration He intends. Notice, however, that the promise of all things being made to work for our good is restricted to "those who love God," which by Jesus' definition means those who obey Him.[5] To fully reap the benefits of restoration we have to choose to obey God's command of *full forgiveness*. This is a great and gracious incentive for releasing the past into His Hands:

> **We know that all things work together for good for those who love God, to those who are called according to his purpose.**
> Romans 8:28 WEB

Recognize and resist the temptation to judgment. God separates us from our sins (see Chapter 5), but judgment *binds* our spirit with bitterness and *blinds* us to our own prideful and unloving hearts. The Holy Spirit gives discernment about sin so that we won't walk in the dark, not knowing good from evil or right from wrong. With proper discernment we can pray for people who are sinning and help them regain their freedom by speaking the truth in love. The enemy, however, desires to turn discernment into judgment. Such bitter judgments are the nature of Satan's kingdom, not God's.

Forgiveness is necessary for our own hearts. The truth is no one is ever trapped in their pain by the sins of others. We are entrapped by our own sin of bitter judgments. We actually imprison our own hearts. Forgiveness brings release! It is a major key to the Kingdom of God (see Chapter 3). We are to loose sinners from their sins and bind the enemy. Sadly, when believers bind sinners to their sins, we unwittingly loose the real enemy and advance his kingdom—first in us, then into the world around us as we spread the poison. Turn the key that sets captive hearts free!

What Forgiveness Is Not

Compare these six common misconceptions to your own beliefs.

1) It is *not* a feeling: Forgiveness is a choice, an act of the will, not a feeling. We cannot control our feelings, but we can control how we choose to respond despite our feelings.

2) It is *not* glossing over: Forgiveness does not pretend the offense was not as bad as it really was. It does not turn a blind eye to real faults. It sees sin as sin and then forgives the person.

3) It is *not* nursing the fond memory: Real forgiveness does not keep score, hold grudges, or build walls. It is necessary to watch our boundaries, but not to build walls on them!

4) It is *not* a reward: Christian forgiveness is not something earned by being sorry or by efforts to change. The less deserved it is, the more it is Christlike, mercy-based forgiveness.

5) It is *not* a divine pardon: Forgiveness is not letting the other person "off the hook"; it is taking them off our hook and putting them in God's Hands for redemption. Trust Him!

6) It is *not* blindly trusting: Forgiveness creates no obligation to trust the offender. Jesus trusted Himself to no one, but He lived in forgiveness and love with everyone. He still does. Aren't you glad He forgives you, even though He can't trust you never to betray his love? Let's learn to do likewise.

So what exactly does forgiveness involve? Forgiveness means being open to loving and even liking the other person, accepting them just as they are—just as we would desire to be accepted and loved if we were them. It means releasing them, setting them free, letting them go, letting them be themselves and setting our own hearts free in the process. *Forgiveness is giving your pain and the injustice to God and trusting Him with it.* It will always liberate you!

Five Biblical Motivations to Forgive

Try these motivations for leverage, they really work.

1) Your own freedom: Unforgiveness brings torment by binding hurt, hardness and heaviness to our hearts.[6] It also generates fear and insecurity and it is a block to receiving answers to prayers, even prayers for healing.

2) They don't know what they are doing: Because Jesus said it, we know it's true. Let it work for you.[7] Everyone who sins has been deceived by an invisible enemy.

104

3) Humble yourself: See Jesus dying on the cross for you and it is easier to release others.[8] See your own sin of bitterness for what it is and you will immediately be humbled.

4) Get compassion for them: God looks past the sin to see the wounds. Do likewise.[9] Everyone who sins came into the world as an infant just wanting to be loved. Something went wrong.

5) Let Jesus gain the inheritance He died to receive—forgiveness for all sinners: He wants *everyone* forgiven and in heaven.

Prepare your heart to forgive. The first stage in gaining victory is recognizing the spiritual problem and being willing to take full responsibility for having it. The problem in this case is the sin of unforgiveness! The second stage is praying for God to help you with it, casting the burden on Him to do it in you, through you and for you. The third stage is coming into obedience with what the Lord shows you that you need to do.

The Way to Freedom

Usually it is not difficult to discern when we are holding hurt or a hardened heart against someone, only to release the "death grip" we may have on them for the hurt or offense. But avoidance of dealing with past pains and doing the hard work of forgiving is a very real threat to ever gaining our true freedom. Be determined! If you break a hard job down, it's easier to do. Really go to work with these ten steps and they will work for you. Bring the five motivations in and power up! Set your will to agree with God and let Him take your heart on a pilgrimage to new life.[10] If at first you don't succeed, don't give up. The Lord loves to reward those who persevere. You really can do this—with His help.

1) Seek grace: Ask God to help you by the power of His Spirit to make a real commitment of your will to do His will. If you really want to obey Him, then He will empower you.

2) Acknowledge the pain: Sin hurts. God grieved for you and has grieved with you, but comfort alone will not heal you.

3) Ask God to forgive them: Really mean it. He already does, but you need to express it and set His mercy in motion.

4) Ask God to catch the thief and make him pay: Commit the real enemy (Satan's kingdom) to God for His justice.[11]

5) Ask God to forgive you (for judging them): Believe that He has and be ready to share with them the grace you just received.

6) Choose to forgive them: Pray it and say it by an act of your will; put your heart in it: "By an act of my will, I choose to release you from all my bitter judgments…"

7) Choose to forgive yourself (for prolonging the pain): Accept it. Release the pain. Command the "tormentors" to go.

8) Choose to believe God's promise of redemption is for you (Romans 8:28): Rejoice in restoration and blessings to come.

9) Pray for them: Pray for them to receive all of the blessings you would like God to bestow on you.[12]

10) Thank God by faith for His wisdom and goodness in what He allows: Re-surrender and resubmit to His leadership.

God is seeking a people after His own Heart—a people willing to keep their hearts open and loving, no matter what the cost. Don't pass up this opportunity to become a grace giver. It begins as an act of the will. Feelings follow. Experience the peace and release of finally letting go. Say *Yes!* to life.

Lord, help me want what You want (forgiveness) and hate what You hate (un-forgiveness). I would rather be free on the inside, than bitter. I will set free anyone I have to in order to get free. What was done to me is nothing compared to what bitterness is doing to me now. I am not bound by the past, only by my bitterness about it. Whatever the reasons are for being bitter, they are not as good as freedom feels. I will turn the key of forgiveness and walk away. I therefore choose to forgive _____ and release him/her from all my bitter judgments. I am giving ____ to You along with all the pain and injustice for You to redeem. I am trusting You with it all. Thank You for forgiving me for being so unforgiving!

CHAPTER 16

MENDING THE BROKEN HEART

The Stronghold of Trauma

Almost everyone knows what it is like to carry the wounds of unhealed traumas of the past. Like the physical cuts and bruises that we try to shield from further damage, these are memories that we don't want to touch on in conversation or can only talk about very carefully because so much pain still remains. Some things have happened, large or small, that hurt us and broke our trust with God, self or others. As long as there is pain in the memory, our heart is still broken by those incidents and the distrust and fears that assail us have reason to remain.[1] Unhealed trauma will always make our world seem unsafe to our emotions.

Ironically, the safest life to have is not one that can't be broken by painful events but one which is quickly restored by releasing full forgiveness to others and steadfastly trusting in God despite the pain God allows. Don't believe me? Then ask Jesus. It is the way that He lived; it is the Way He invites us to follow.[2] Every harrowing passage through the cross of unwanted pain will carry us into a resurrection of New Creation life—if we do not lose hope (see The Disciple's Cross in Postscripts). God never afflicts us with trauma—He doesn't author evil—but He will use it to grow a heart in us like that of Jesus. *Isn't that what we really want?* To become more like Him. In the end we will all be thanking God for the suffering that prepared us for a greater "weight of glory"—why not embrace heaven's perspective now?[3]

What Are Traumas?

For the purpose of this series, trauma is considered to be any event of the past from which we are still carrying pain, broken trust, and/or unresolved negative emotions. Consider these definitions of trauma taken from *Webster's College Dictionary*[4]:

1) A body wound or shock produced by physical injury.

2) Psychological shock or severe distress from experiencing a disastrous event outside the range of usual experience, as rape, military combat, or an airplane crash.

3) Any wrenching or distressing experience.

Traumas often become doors through which the enemy enters to plant distortions of the truth and to bind the heart with bitterness, fear and soul-killing messages. These wounded areas can grow into strongholds—areas of our flesh that are well-fortified against the life of the Spirit and are hard for us to overcome. Traumatic events such as illness, accidents and abuse may also have been points of entry for evil spirits. Traumas engender a legacy of fears that follow us into adulthood: phobias, dreads, our characteristic set of semi-irrational dislikes and anxieties, as well as bitter feelings of regret, resentment and shame. Lies the enemy has planted hound us throughout life, such as: "You're not wanted; you're no good; you'll never make it." Additionally, we tend to define ourselves by what has happened to us in the past, rather than by the new identity and the bright future that God says is ours forever.

We always have a choice how we will respond to each moment or event in life. The enemy takes unfair advantage of our innocence and ignorance to subvert the choices we make, but they are still *our* choices. Without sufficient knowledge of God and His ways we may have reacted in a wrong manner to what was done to us. This is "only natural" (allowing fallen nature to guide us) and all too common. Yet, such ungodly reactions to trauma are what bring the curse upon us. We may have reacted in ignorance of God's ways, but we are still responsible for decisions we made, attitudes we formed, any acting out we did, or any inner vows we may have made. Thankfully, there is real hope! We have a God who knows how to deliver us out of *all* our afflictions. His ways really work—as we learn to cooperate.

Many are the afflictions of the righteous, but the Lord delivers him out of them all. Psalm 34:19

Preliminary Steps towards Healing

Jesus is a mansion builder in our soul, yet many live in the dungeon of what should be their mansion—locked in a dark room with terrible memories, devastated by trauma, bound by bitterness. It's rightly said by A.A. that we are as sick as our secrets—for darkness is the enemy's domain.[5] Tragically, the very things we hide from God and others are the things He wants to heal. If we truly want to be free, we will have to honestly and openly deal with past trauma so that the root of fear, hurt or bitterness can be removed, and make ourselves trusting and vulnerable to those God would use as instruments of His healing. We will have to risk exposing our wounds to the Light of Christ in the presence of the people He appoints (discerning who to trust). But not all at once! Think of issues like tissues in a box and let the Lord pull them out one at a time. God wants to mend your broken heart as time goes on, but you have to give Him all of the pieces. Hold nothing back.

It was prophesied of the Messiah that He would mend broken hearts. At the start of His ministry Jesus read from this text of Isaiah in which that promise had been given.[6] This ministry of Jesus has never ended. He still comes to heal the brokenhearted.

> **"The Spirit of the Lord God is upon me, because the Lord has anointed me to bring good news to the poor; he has sent me to bind up the brokenhearted, proclaim liberty to the captives, and the opening of the prison to those who are bound; to proclaim the year of the Lord's favor."** Isaiah 61:1-2

To pursue our freedom we will have to learn how to recognize the thoughts of trauma. Usually we are aware of the traumatic events of our past, but sometimes we can live in unconscious denial, having lost touch with the reality of how much we were hurt in the past. Because we have been given free will, if we do not freely choose to bring our wounded places to the Lord, He will not be in a position to mend them. Hence, it is important that we keep ourselves sensitive to what the Holy Spirit may want to show us. Traumas may be carried by us in three main ways:

1) Painfully obvious: Often we are aware of the traumatic events of our past and still carry them with us like raw wounds that throb with pain whenever we think back upon them. We have carried them so long that it seems like we have been permanently damaged by them—but that is a lie of the enemy. God can and does heal even the deepest traumas.

2) Partially buried: Some traumas are so painful that we shove them down and spend a lot of mental energy keeping them submerged. Some of the worst traumas are forcefully forgotten until present events bring memories to the surface or trigger the powerful negative emotions they contain.

3) Hidden in plain sight: There are other events that we have glossed over so thoroughly that they no longer seem to bother us, but it spills out of us in conversation through stories we keep repeating.[7] Or we may feel fine until someone begins to pry and poke into these memories. The emotions that come out of us are the best indicators of what is still hidden in our hearts.[8]

Five Ways God Heals Trauma

There are five main ways that God heals trauma. Note that these are not automatic. They all require a good deal of cooperation on our part, including knowledge (recognition of the trauma) and motivation (a persevering desire to see it mended). If it were otherwise, everyone would be free. We need to become determined to aggressively seek the freedom from the past and entry into His Kingdom that God wants to give us.[9] Carry your traumatic experiences into these five proven ways of mending:

1) Our tears: There is a blessing on those who carry their grief to God and give it to Him. Think of tears as liquid prayers. In the Sermon on the Mount Jesus said that there is actually a blessing on those who mourn—God promises to comfort us.[10] It may not be easy at first, but all of us can learn to grieve over past losses and still maintain a heart of faith that knows God is listening to our cry and will use our tears and prayers to mend our hearts and restore bright hope to our future.[11]

2) The prayers of others: James tells us that we must confess to one another if we want to be healed.[12] This is especially true of emotional wounds. The enemy will try to use embarrassment or shame to stop you. Don't let him! Be willing to be open, honest and vulnerable with close Christian friends or ministers that you can entrust with your heart. God wants to use the Body of

Christ as an instrument of His healing. This keeps us humbled and dependent upon one another and it also helps rebuild the trust in others which trauma damaged.

3) Forgiveness: Giving grace always clears the way for prayers to be answered and life to be restored. Forgiveness is absolutely necessary.[13] It is even more important for our healing than learning how to release our tears to the Lord or confess to our friends because unforgiveness is the number one block to seeing our prayers answered (Chapter 15).

4) Believing truth: The promise of total restoration is a true godsend.[14] A fully restored life would not be possible without this gift of love. It means that the Lord has purposed to overturn anything the enemy has done to rob us (whether it was the result of our own sin or someone else's) and bring about a greater good so that our joy in Him can know no bounds. Once you unite your faith to the truth of what He has promised you, the Holy Spirit ignites a believing heart inside you. Such *living* faith produces joy in you over what is now coming your way, rather than sorrow and regret over your losses (Chapter 13). Why keep holding on to what you cannot repair? Give it to Him in complete confidence that His Word is true and that He will not fail to fulfill it.

> **And we know that for those who love God all things work together for good, for those who are called according to his purpose.** Romans 8:28

5) Divine intervention: Dreams, visions, healing of memories, visitations and prophetic words are supernatural operations of the Holy Spirit which we can position ourselves to receive by worshipping and fellowshipping in environments where such manifestations are welcomed and encouraged.

> **I will pour out my Spirit on all flesh; your sons and your daughters shall prophesy, your old men shall dream dreams, and your young men shall see visions.** Joel 2:28

Full healing of trauma is possible! No trauma has been fully healed if it still hurts to remember any part of it, or if patterns that began after the trauma happened are still continuing. Yet fully forgiving all who need to be forgiven and fully receiving forgiveness where we need it brings us to the place where there is no pain attached to any of the memories. Jesus heals the brokenhearted—especially as we forgive.

The Way to Freedom

Deeper wounds from trauma often call for a longer journey of cleansing and healing. Don't despair! There is much growth all along the way towards the final resolution and lifting of the pain. Like the pangs of childbirth, the pain of the recovery process will always appear "slight" once you come out on the other side, basking in the freshness and delight of new life.

1) First, become willing to face the pain, praying for faith that God really can take you through to the other side where healing abounds and for the strength to go the distance with Him.

2) On your own or with the help of a trusted spiritual friend, do the work of fully forgiving *from the heart* anyone who hurt you or sinned against you.

3) Take full responsibility for any acting out you did: Repent, renounce and carry those unloving ways captive to Christ, falling totally out of agreement with any false beliefs as well.

4) Turn to the Father and release gratitude to Him that He loves you and fully intends to overturn every evil with a greater good!

Father, You have given me this promise of total redemption so it must be true; You have commanded me to forgive everyone so that must be what needs to happen for my life to be healed and restored. I choose by an act of my will to forgive the people in my past who have hurt me or wronged me, including myself. I release them from all my bitter judgments and give them to You for You to redeem. I also repent of my unbelief in Your Word and now choose by an act of my will to believe that the promise of Romans 8:28 is true for me—that greater good will come out of my past than all of the pain and loss the enemy sowed into it. I choose to believe in You!

CHAPTER 17

ACCEPTED IN THE BELOVED

The Stronghold of Rejection

Traumatic experiences easily sow feelings of rejection within us, especially if these were sins of verbal, physical or sexual abuse directed against us. In fact every sin against us is a form of rejection, even the well-meaning, conditional love of parents and teachers who put their approval of us on a performance basis. Although perfect love must at times reject behavior and attitudes that are not right, the person we are deep down is always loved by God. To be rejected (for who we are) by the looks, words or deeds of others is a tremendously painful, traumatic experience.

Many people—the shy, the perfectionists, the exhibitionists, the high achievers—organize their whole lives around trying to avoid rejection by others, while seeking to gain their approvals. The math on this is terrible: Have you noticed that ten approvals can be easily wiped out by one rejection? Sadly, the pain of *possible* rejection keeps millions hiding their true self from others (even from God), running from real intimacy, love and life into the safer, shallow waters of meaningless relationships and purposeless lives. Rejection is an ugly stronghold in the land promised to us that must be brought down!

The Antidote for Rejection

Begin wrapping your heart and your life around this astounding truth: Our Father will never reject or forsake us.[1] From before the worlds were created He has loved us and desired us. *We are secure in Him.* This is the antidote for any rejection we feel. The Father's total and unalterable acceptance is the Fact upon which the joy of our new life is based: Because of His great love for us, He sent Jesus to the cross to atone for all of our sins and has even given His Spirit to help us believe in the grace He wants us to receive.

Blessed be the God and Father of our Lord Jesus Christ...According as he hath chosen us in him before the foundation of the world...

Having predestinated us unto the adoption of children by Jesus Christ to himself... wherein he hath made us accepted in the beloved. Ephesians 1:3-6 KJV

People, on the other hand, can and will reject and forsake us. Rejection by others is extremely painful to experience whenever we are secretly looking to other people to declare our worth to us. However, if our hearts had been established in God's love for us, as Jesus' was, we could have handled the pain of rejection every bit as well as He did. Fortunately, it is never too late to learn! Let the pain of rejection that you have experienced drive you to fastening your heart on what *God* says about you, not on what *people* say. God's view of you is the truth that will set you free.[2] Fight to fall out of agreement with the compelling power of the enemy's beliefs about you. Learn to resist the lion's roar and the serpent's venom![3]

Considering what rejection is made of, it is no wonder that it is so painful to feel. So, what is rejection?[4] These are its major parts:

1) It plays an integral role in all mental and emotional illness, since it is very damaging to our sense of self.

2) It is a terrible lie. There may be sin in us worth rejecting, but we are not sin and are never meant to be rejected (Chapter 5).

3) It is a sin against us. God has commanded everyone to love and accept us as He does.[5] He commands you to love and accept *all* of them, right? They are under the same command.

4) It is an evil spirit—one that delights to feel and express rejection in us and towards others.

5) It becomes *our own sin* of unbelief in God and idolatry of others, whenever we agree with it.

Did you get that last point? The sin of receiving rejection and agreeing with it is the real source of all the pain. The pain of being rejected hurts when it hits us, but holding on to it allows the torment to continue, like a "death-grip" on an exposed electric wire that was touched *while being improperly grounded*. We need to learn how to let go *and* get better grounding![6]

Rejection can also open doors for the enemy to bring even more pain and problems upon us through the fear of man and through self-rejection (see Lesson 18). How little did we realize that in seeking people's approvals, we were subtly being trained by an unseen enemy in the ways of *idolatry*. By trying to get our worth affirmed through others, rather than through God, we began making other people's opinions into a god to us. Have we become "addicted" to approval by others? Thank God, this is not held against us and we can begin to find freedom by recognizing sin as sin and turning from our idolatry of others' opinions to instead live by what God declares about us. [7]

Turning from that false god will leave us sorely lacking a sense of worth unless we can stir our faith to truly trust in and rely upon the acceptance our Father is giving us every moment of the day. It is here that we may encounter another problem—our *unbelief* in God. In any moment we could have joy, confidence, and assurance of acceptance imparted to us by our loving Father, but He gives it through our faith in His Word and not very often as a feeling. Faith is like an electric tool—it does little good unless it is plugged into a "live" electrical current. We need to plug what we believe about God into the current of a living faith. To do this we may first have to confess that the sin of unbelief has been capturing our heart and learn to walk by faith, not feeling.[8]

The truth is that the pain of rejection, as terrible as it is, can actually help us if we learn to let it turn us away from the wrong direction we keep trying to go with our hearts. All along, our hearts were only meant to be "plugged in" to God. The pain of rejection is like touching a hot stove. Let's learn the lesson and turn away from what burns us and live by what gives life.

The Secret Snares of Rejection

There is a "secret knowledge" that snares us. Rejection plays into a painful inner sense that already makes us feel insecure—the knowledge of indwelling sin. Even as children we may have known that something was wrong on the inside, though we would likely not have been able to articulate it. The terrible truth about our fallenness is that for our sins and separation from God, we should all be rejected. Our sinfulness actually deserves hell—the ultimate rejection. Yet, this truth of who we are *apart from Christ* is meant to be swallowed up by the greater truth of the gospel: Jesus suffered rejection and abandonment by God on our behalf so that we would *never* have to experience it. The gospel liberates us from the torment of rejection—if we believe it with our whole heart.

Unchecked by a living faith, rejection creates unhealthy defense mechanisms. These failed coping strategies are ways of the fallen nature we may have used to defend ourselves against rejection when it happened to us, whether it was real or imagined. We may have been only half-aware or completely unaware of what we were doing—no doubt it seemed the best way to handle it at the time. Nevertheless, these ungodly patterns now imprison us behind walls that keep the lovely, New Creation side of ourselves from emerging. Did any of these strategies gain a strong hold on you?[9]

1) Withdrawal: Retreating like a turtle into its shell in order to avoid rejection. Remedy: Believe God for His acceptance of you, keep your eyes on Him and stay in the game.

2) Anger and hatred: Rejecting others when hurt by rejection. Remedy: Forgive everyone from the heart and you won't be carrying around so much anger.

3) False identity: Searching for an identity other than who we are in Christ. Remedy: Trust and obey Jesus so that the Holy Spirit can unfold your true personality.[10]

4) Perfectionism: Trying to avoid possible rejection by becoming "bullet proof" against criticism. Beware: If you live by the approval of others, you will "die" by their disapproval. Remedy: Fasten your heart to the grace that God covers you with, living under *His* leadership, not your own demands.

Rejection often leads to self-rejection, a deceptive and very destructive snare. Spirits of self-rejection want you convinced that you are unworthy, unacceptable, unlovable, and that's why you're being rejected. No! Rejection is *always* the other person's sin, not yours. In listening to and agreeing with it you open yourself up to hating and rejecting yourself. The more you reject yourself, the more you become afraid that God and everyone you meet will also reject you. This amplifies the pain and the problem. Soon you may be feeling rejected *even when you aren't*.

Never forget the truth from Ephesians that your Father loved you long before He created you. You are no accident! He made you someone He can and does love wholeheartedly. Let *that* reality capture your heart—not the opinions of sinful mortals (including yourself). You are fully accepted, totally unique, unconditionally loved and forever embraced. You won the "spiritual lottery." By grace alone you are destined to live in endless joy. God's mind is made up! He wants you! So, don't listen to the whispers of a spirit of rejection or let it cast a shadow on God's feelings for you. You are an awesome work of His Hands and Heart.[11]

Jesus and Rejection

Jesus knows what rejection is. He experienced rejection as a man for our sake throughout His life, His ministry and especially in His dying. At the cross He felt the full force of rejection first come *against* Him (as He was rejected and sentenced to death) and then *enter* within Him (as our sins and their rightful punishment came upon Him).[12] He was made to *be* sin so that we could be freely given right standing with God and *never* be rejected.[13] He bore it all at the cross in His innermost being—He knows how awful it feels and how deadly it is. He fully sympathizes.[14] Jesus also bore the rejection of the Father. In the final moments on the cross His mournful cry of dereliction revealed that He was experiencing the full penalty of sin that was due to us—the utter abandonment by God to death, separation and judgment upon sin.[15] He spared us from *ever* having to experience that ultimate agony.

Spirits of rejection lie against the truth. They want you to feel rejected, unworthy, inferior and insecure. The truth is that you have very real spiritual enemies who despise you and who will always seek to make you feel rejected, but you don't have to think what they think or feel what they feel. You can learn to rest your heart in God who will never abandon you or reject you.[16]

Learn to stop touching the hot stove of letting others declare to you your worth (turn from the idolatry of others). Put your whole heart into what He says He sees when He looks your way (seek to defeat all unbelief). The first step to freedom from any sinful pattern is recognizing the sin or the evil spirit that needs to be dealt with as not being the real you and then dealing with it accordingly. You are already accepted and saved by God, so don't take no for an answer. Say "No!" to thoughts of rejection instead. Jesus is God's "Yes!" to you (His Name is _Yeshua_ in Hebrew).[17]

The Way to Freedom

Usually the pain of being rejected is easy to recognize as someone's sin against us, but the reality of our own sinful grip on those feelings of rejection is much harder to see and comprehend. Defeating feelings of rejection requires dedication to God's truth.

1) In the midst of the painful feelings, begin declaring forgiveness for the person who rejected you, repenting of the idolatry of putting their opinion about you above God's.

2) Repent for taking the message of rejection to heart, carrying those thoughts captive and repenting of unbelief until you recover faith that God's acceptance of you is all you really need.

3) Turn to the Father and release gratitude to Him that He loves you perfectly and accepts you always—*just as you are!*

Father, forgive me for holding out my heart to other people to declare my worth to me. You have declared Your unending love for me and my eternal worth to You by sending Jesus to the cross. Forgive me for letting other people's opinions matter to me more than Your own. I repent of and renounce all rejection I have ever taken on. It is not about what they did or said—it is all about my unwitting sin of holding on to it—and letting them be god to me. By an act of my will I am taking my heart back from others and giving it to You. May I only desire to see me through Your eyes. Thank You for Your steadfast love and acceptance. My heart is safe under the covering of Your perfect love and Your promise to never leave me or forsake me.

CHAPTER 18

LOVE THYSELF!

The Stronghold of Self-Rejection

In the previous chapter we explored the emotional damage that rejection by others can cause and the effective remedy of faith in our Father's perfect love and acceptance. Not knowing our true security in God, when others rejected us, the power of that pain may have carried us into rejecting ourselves. Yet, unless we truly believe in our heart of hearts that it is a great, good thing to be who we are *just as we are*, we have been robbed of a major part of our glorious inheritance in Christ. Did you know that Jesus actually expects us to love and accept ourselves—*just as He does*? Why else would He take proper love of self as a standard for loving others?

> **And he said to him, "You shall love the Lord your God with all your heart and with all your soul and with all your mind.' This is the great and first commandment. And a second is like it: 'You shall love your neighbor as yourself.'"** Matthew 22:37-39

These words of Jesus carry a curious fulfillment. We are to love our neighbors *as* we love ourselves. But what if we don't love ourselves? Not loving ourselves will limit and set obstacles to truly loving others. And it happens in this way: If I am angry with myself, it will spill out onto others as frustration with them. If I haven't learned to receive mercy for myself, I will become judgmental of others. If I cannot entrust my life to God, I will tend to become fearful for and controlling of the ones I love. If I am critical towards myself, I will tend to be critical of others. This cycle goes on and on because the sad truth is that even though we try to manage it, make up for it or cover it up, we can only love others *as* we love ourselves. So, let's learn to give grace to ourselves, *rightly* love ourselves in Christ and become grace givers to others!

A Worthwhile Life Lesson

Worthwhile life lessons don't come easily. For many of us the ultimate challenge of the truly converted Christian life is learning to love the sinner and hate the sin. Would you believe that to help us God has assigned a problem-prone sinner to each one of us? By "sneaky" design He has placed in all our lives someone for us to get to know intimately, someone whose weaknesses, failings and stupidities cause us no end of trouble. Yet, we are fully expected to learn how to love that sinner unconditionally, while still holding a perfect hatred for all the sins. Look no further, that sinner is you! You the sinner is joined at the hip to you the New Creation—*oh my God!* It's time to come to conversion about the gospel applied to ourselves. To see how much work may be needed, take this test to determine how well you give grace to yourself. Can you apply 1 Corinthians 13:4-8 (the "love chapter") to yourself?[1]

> Are you harder on yourself than on others? Do you berate yourself?
> Get angry with yourself easily? Depression counts as self-anger!
> Are there things about yourself that you dislike and can't accept?
> Are there things in your past that you just can't forgive yourself for?
> How do you talk to yourself when you have done something stupid?
>
> *If you answered yes, why would you think treating yourself this way is normal? It may be common like a cold but it is not a healthy normal.*

Accepting the "Unacceptable"

There are many things about us that God is at peace with but which we still fear and hate. In fact He seems to be in no hurry to make change come in these areas. Not being reconciled to God about these things can keep us striving against ourselves. Complete self-acceptance is the grace-filled starting point for entering into God's good plans for our life. Provided that we have repented where necessary, He is always the One who completely accepts us just as we are and is willing to lead us into new life. *We* are the holdouts who cannot accept our lives as they are and resist living on His terms. Make sure you can accept all nine of these things about yourself *without reservation*. God already does! Become fully reconciled to the God who is already reconciled to you.

We implore you on behalf of Christ, be reconciled to God.
2 Corinthians 5:20

1) Past hurtful events: We need to see that the Father grieved over pain and injustice coming into our lives, but God is a realist. He has had to accept that all manner of pain had to be allowed because free will is allowed. So God grieves, but He is also ready, willing and able to lead anyone into a life in which evil is overturned and made to work for good. Such living begins on the other side of acceptance. At the very least accept that it happened and be willing to go on with God. Even better, vigorously thank God by faith for all you have been through.

2) Failures, wrong choices: No one wants to fail and make wrong choices, but we all do. God allows us to experience failure in order for us to learn from our mistakes things we evidently could not learn by the truths He has shown us. He will never reproach us; instead He will help us gain and grow.[2] The only one who really fails is the one who doesn't keep trying, the one who doesn't persevere.[3] Don't live with a fear of failure: Repent, receive grace, push delete and get going again!

3) Weaknesses/foolishness: Because we receive so much affirmation from others over our strengths, we often tend to concentrate our efforts there and build a sense of self-worth around things we do well. Let your perspective shift on this one. Our strengths are God's gifts to us; trusting Him with our weaknesses is our gift to Him. For most of us it wasn't our strengths that brought us to Christ, but our weaknesses. Our weaknesses grow our prayer life, increase humility in us and compassion for others, and remind us to depend upon God for his help. His strength and grace are perfected in us through the very weaknesses we despise.[4] Don't try to be weak, but when you see your weaknesses, choose to look upon them as "tutors" and "spiritual guides" leading you closer to Christ.[5]

4) Lack of knowledge: We often seek knowledge out of a misguided desire to cover ourselves by being right. But it is not knowledge that covers us, it is Jesus' Blood and God's love. It is not knowledge as information that saves us, it is *knowing God* in trust and intimacy. The humble truth is that we are hugely ignorant of both the world of information and the vast Infinity that is God. Let pride take the hit: Admit your boundless

ignorance as a finite, fallen creature, then acknowledge that you know One who will never fault you for it, but will graciously share His wisdom with you.[6]

5) Family heritage: It's too late. God made the call and didn't consult you. Take it on faith that God chose your heritage for reasons of the blessings—not the curses—that are in your generations and the divine purposes that will fulfill your life.[7]

6) Present limitations: At times we probably have all hated our limits, whether of age, intelligence, appearance or abilities. God will likely grow us beyond many present limitations as we "wait upon Him" in faith, but in the meantime rest with peace and acceptance, trusting His unlimited abilities.[8]

7) Personality and patterns: This is tricky because if you are reading this book you may want some of your personality and patterns changed so that the New Creation life can come forth—never buy into an aspect of yourself as being the real you if it doesn't match up with Jesus *in you*, right? (Good you're learning!) But what we don't want is to hold our breath as we wait for those changes to come. For example, if shyness has been a personality pattern, confess it as the fear of man, then cast the burden of freeing you from it on the Lord and take your peace back. The next time shyness tries to rise up be prepared to fight to not let it stop you and eventually it will lose its grip.

8) Your fallen nature: You didn't ask for it. It is not even your fault that you have it. It is in you because of Adam's sin. That's why it's called *Adam's* nature. God isn't asking you to get rid of it—Paul never got rid of his. In fact God has no plan to remove it *down here*: It comes off when we die. While we live it serves a good purpose by keeping us humble and dependent upon Him, grateful that we are covered by the Blood and by the love, and less prideful towards others. What He is saying is this: "Just, don't get dressed up in it and walk around in that old nature!"

9) Physical appearance: The truth about physical appearance is that anyone who has truly put on Christ (in love and delight) has such inner beauty shining out of them that it never fails to transform even the most ordinary countenance. A heart fully

yielded to Christ is the best "make up" in the world and all it costs in this context is casting down vain concerns about how we look outwardly.[9] God looks deep inside and loves us. Let's learn to do it His way.

The Battle Is Over Believing Truth

Son or daughter of Adam, "Who told you that you were naked?"[10] We, too, may feel exposed and vulnerable in our fallenness, but our God is covering us! Are you listening to what God's Word says or are you listening to your feelings, your understanding, your circumstances, or your past failures? Let God alone be your source of truth and recognize every contrary thought as a lie, *even if it comes from you*.[11] Self-rejection is a double snare, because if I reject myself or my life, I am also rejecting the One who created me and is redeeming me. I may be completely unaware of this dynamic, but if I hate my life, I'm saying in effect that the Lord is doing a sloppy job of leading me towards the joy He has promised. That cannot be! God knows what He is doing and His ways of leading us are saturated with His wisdom and love. We simply must learn to admit that we don't have the proper perspective and then choose to see the whole of our life through God's eyes. Heaven's perspective on your life is the one you want.[12]

There is one who hates you and will never cease from faulting you and putting you down. You don't have to listen to him! Neither do you have to listen to yourself. It is a devious form of pride *in us* that demands perfection *from us*—never the Lord who knows that we can "do nothing" apart from the grace He supplies.[13] Such striving grew out of a fear of displeasing others and a wrong image of the Father. Trying to be perfect, or to always be right, is the vain belief that we can cover ourselves with our own good intentions and best efforts—a modern form of works righteousness. This inevitably feeds frustration which can then become very damaging to our physical health by producing the auto-immune diseases.[14] Somehow self-rejection sends a message to our immune system that we are the enemy it needs to attack.

Beware also of how self-rejection is held in place by self-pity. Self-pity only wants to wallow in what has been wrong; it never wants to climb out of the morass of the past. It has been called the "super-glue of hell."[15] Why waste time on those lies? Being saved by God through Christ means that we are of all people *not to be pitied*; we have a God who saves, delivers, prospers, heals and provides—all according to our real needs being watched over by His love and wisdom for us. Are you prepared to recover your life from all past agreements with the enemy's invisible kingdom? You have to be willing to fight to be free, but your God will train you for the battle![16] Live according to your future not your past.[17] God is not going to quit working with you until you are as full of joy over your life with Him as He is.[18]

The Way to Freedom

The difficult thing to recognize about self-rejection is that you are always the person God wants you to be and that you—in your right mind—would want to be, if only you had His perspective. Don't let your pain, problems and sins tell you otherwise!

1) Recognize every thought or feeling of self-rejection, self-frustration, or self-condemnation as coming from the enemy—not God and not the true you.

2) Take full responsibility for agreeing with it: Repent, renounce and carry it captive to Christ until you see something in Him that restores your confidence that God's mercy, love, good plans and the promise of Romans 8:28 are all for you!

3) Turn to the Father and release gratitude to Him that He loves and accepts you even when you don't. Then cast that devil out!

Because of my Father's perfect love for me, His never-ending mercy for me, the future and hope He has for me, and His commitment to bring good out of everything that has ever happened or will ever happen to me, it really is a great, good thing to be me! I therefore choose to fully forgive myself and accept myself—just as He does. And I will fight to take my life back from all unloving attitudes against myself. I may have had a bad beginning, but I am going to have a great never-ending!

CHAPTER 19

GODLY CONTENTMENT

The Stronghold of Envy

Not receiving a fullness of assurance that we are loved, that we belong and that our lives therefore hold great meaning and purpose, leaves us prey for the undercutting work of envy and jealousy. Envy and jealousy scream out: "They are getting what I need and deserve!" Sure it is black-hearted, but it is also revealing of a deep-seated pain and an invisible reality: All of us have been robbed. None of us are getting what we desperately need and were meant to have. The enemy came in through Adam's sin and stole from every child what God desired them to receive, even from the moment of conception. All of us were blocked at birth by Adam's nature from knowing in the depth of our spirits that we are totally loved, fully forgiven, completely accepted by our grace-giving Father. The spiritual "umbilical cord" that was meant to connect us to God's loving Heart was severed by the Fall.

This deep void cannot be fully filled even by the best of parents and fairest of treatment and it leaves all of us exposed to the temptations of envy and jealousy. New birth through faith in Christ restores the missing connection, but old emotional habits are hard to break. We who believe in Christ are inheritors of riches beyond our wildest dreams.[1] However, we may still be held captive by the old feelings of deprivation and former patterns of striving to get "our fair share." St. Francis is credited with saying that he who expects nothing "can enjoy everything."[2] That may well be true, but only if he (or she) has first dealt with the stronghold of envy.

The Superior Power of Contentment

Godly contentment is our graced antidote for the poison of envy and jealousy. Whenever this stronghold seeks to snare you, quickly search out Jesus to restore your sense of contentment as His well-beloved child. Paul says that godly contentment was something that he gained as he grew. We can learn it too.

> Not that I am speaking of being in need, for I have learned in whatever situation I am to be content. I know how to be brought low, and I know how to abound. In any and every circumstance, I have learned the secret of facing plenty and hunger, abundance and need. Philippians 4:11-12

Contentment is actually great gain. It brings with it the peace which "surpasses all understanding," a peace that is truly out of this world.[3] It removes fruitless and disturbing anxieties and replaces them with a gentle fullness. Contentment is safe to desire because we can never have too much of it.

> Now there is great gain in godliness with contentment, for we brought nothing into the world, and we cannot take anything out of the world. But if we have food and clothing, with these we will be content. But those who desire to be rich fall into temptation, into a snare. 1 Timothy 6:6-9

The Destructive Power of Envy and Jealousy

Envy and jealousy, on the other hand, keep us stirred up and dis-contented. These spirits keep us thinking about and noticing what others have and what we don't have. Why should this seem so natural? Isn't the Holy Spirit always at work inside of us to help us notice what others don't have (so we can serve them) and what we do have (so we can be thankful and rest contented)? Why is the voice of the enemy so much easier to hear? We need to be much more discerning about which spirit is directing our perceptions. Any upsurge of envy means that we are definitely being robbed of something that we deserve to have, but what the thieves are actually stealing is none other than our godly contentment!

Envy is destructive of our bodies. Bone marrow is crucial to a healthy immune system, but envy weakens it. On the other hand a sound heart is a grateful heart—it gives life to the body.[4]

> The life of the body is a heart at peace, but envy rots the bones. Proverbs 14:30 WEB

Envy is also destructive of the Body of Christ. Much of the strife and conflict in the church comes from jealousy among the members. It is difficult for anyone to be advanced by God or to become especially gifted without envy being set loose to destroy the fellowship. This holds everyone back.

> What causes quarrels and what causes fights among you? Is it not this, that your passions are at war within you? You desire and do not have, so you murder. You covet and cannot obtain, so you fight and quarrel. James 4:1-2

Getting to the Root of the Problem

Envy and jealousy grow out of three roots we would do well to pray against: covetousness, pride and bitterness.

Root #1) Covetousness:[5] To covet is to long for or lust for something that is not yours. Covetousness always wants more—and it wants it right now. Never content with present blessings, it sets us at enmity with others and with God.[6] It is a form of idolatry, since it places things before God and keeps us focused on *getting something from* God, rather than *giving ourselves to* God. As soon as our heart covets something, even a blessing or a spiritual gift, we are putting it ahead of our relationship with Christ and we begin losing our entry into the Kingdom, for that is only supplied to those who seek the Kingdom *first*.[7] Consequently, the Kingdom's peace, joy and power slip through our fingers when we grasp to gain an idol rather than the Lord.[8]

Root #2) Pride:[9] Pride tries to gloss over or fill in the awful sense of not really having what we needed of love and acceptance. As a covering pride cannot help but bring us into conflict with others through competition or comparisons meant to prove to ourselves as well as to others that we are not inferior. We must come off seeming superior at least in our eyes or dissatisfied pride become jealous of their gifts and abilities.

Root #3) Bitterness:[10] Bitterness towards others makes us resentful when they do well or receive blessings. We hate it that they are being shown favor instead of discipline. Self-bitterness, on the other hand, can make us feel that we haven't received what we needed or deserved—and that can lead into self-pity. Either way, if bitter envy is in the heart it is something truly demonic—give it no place!

Beware to compare! When we don't get what we want, we may look around and compare ourselves to others, wanting what they have. You can't win at this: Always some have less, and some have more. Trust God to be measuring out what blessings are truly right and needful for you (and for others) and keep your eyes on Him.

> **Not that we dare to classify or compare ourselves with some of those who are commending themselves. But when they measure themselves by one another and compare themselves with one another, they are without understanding.** 2 Corinthians 10:12

Let's get something straight: Your Father does not play favorites or show partiality.[11] Amazingly, the Father doesn't even love Jesus more than He loves you!

> **I in them and you in me, that they may become perfectly one, so that the world may know that you sent me and loved them even as you loved me.** John 17:23

Our Father is a great provider.[12] The devil plays long and loudly upon our litany of wants, but God faithfully goes about supplying our needs. What's more, He Himself is our "exceedingly great Reward."[13] Be on guard: Envy will never remind you how great a provider your Father is, so ask the Holy Spirit to keep reminding you, and run back to rest contented in your Father's perfect love and loving plans for you—at the first twinge of envy.

> **Keep your life free from love of money, and be content with what you have, for he has said, "I will never leave you nor forsake you."** Hebrews 13:5

Practical Help to Practice

To work at defeating the root of covetousness, try these five practical steps for increasing your trust in God's provision:

1) Tithing. "Returning" the tithe is a faith journey that frees us from being controlled by thinking we are our own providers and opens our eyes to see God's sustaining Hand.[14]

2) Why stop with the tithe? Let "offerings" carry you beyond the tithe. Give at His promptings and watch how God works to keep the river of blessing flowing through you to others.

3) Why just give money back to Him? Whenever we realize that nothing "belongs" to us, everything can be seen as a gift.[15]

4) Let what He provides guide. What God actually provides can guide our decisions about what can be afforded, showing where He draws the line between what we need and what we desire.

5) Practice gratitude for what has already been given. This turns our world around and fills even the seemingly emptiest cups as the "sacrifice" of thanksgiving opens our eyes to see all He already is giving.[16] St. Augustine prayed, "You have given so much to us. Give us one thing more, a grateful heart."[17]

Here is the best practical step of all for defeating a jealous spirit: As soon as you begin feeling envious of another's blessing, vigorously thank God for His provision to them. Get really good at affirming others in their spiritual gifts and at celebrating their victories with them. This totally disarms the enemy (envy), and opens the way for the Lord to extend blessing to you.

Waiting upon the Lord also grows contentment. Many of us have become so accustomed to "instant gratification" as a way of life in the modern world that we easily overlook the value that the scriptures place upon waiting. Waiting on God is a huge subject in the Bible: It includes active faith, bright hope and lively expectancy, combined with patience and perseverance. Without an ability to wait upon the Lord to make the fullness of His provision manifest, we are prey to being captured by envy and jealousy over what we don't have that others do—*in the moment*. However, with this faith ability in place we are actually told that we can possess our souls by patience.[18] Simply by learning patience we can be uplifted, rather than crushed, by whatever is going on in our lives.[19] We can learn how to live for God's Better Day, which He is always leading us towards, on the other side of present troubles or short comings.[20]

There is a great joy in the world of things and in the operation of spiritual gifts, but it is not found in what we can get for ourselves by our own striving. True joy is found in what we see the great God of heaven actually giving to us freely out of His love and care. From this flows endless and deep satisfaction. Everything can come to be seen as a gift of love—both what God provides as well as what He withholds. Through that accurate vision there are such *treasures* of contentment, security and love as to fill even the emptiest of hearts.

The Way to Freedom

Envy and jealousy are thieves that get us chasing in the wrong direction, trying to grasp after blessing, rather than allowing God to bestow all good things in His good time. The tricky part is learning to remember how good godly contentment felt only moments before envy showed up and snatched it from us!

1) Be honest about every false or wrong desire "to grasp" after something you've not yet been given and recognize every twinge of envy as stealing your peace and godly contentment!

2) Take full responsibility for agreeing with it: Repent, renounce and carry it captive to Christ until you see something in Him that restores your confidence in God's provision for you.

3) Turn to the Father and release gratitude to Him for His loving plans to lead you step-by-step into your true inheritance!

Father, forgive me wherever I have doubted your goodness or wisdom in how You have provided for me throughout my life. Forgive me wherever I have sought Your Hand of blessing and failed to seek Your Face of love. Forgive me wherever I have measured Your love by my lack, rather than by the cross where You Yourself willingly suffered loss for my sake. I see Your love now and I cast myself fully and freely upon Your wisdom in what You choose to provide and what You choose to withhold. Let it all work to bring me to that place of incomparable joy where I finally see all elements of my life—even the "missing" ones—as loving gifts from My Beloved.

CHAPTER 20

EXPOSING THE DARKNESS

The Stronghold of the Occult

At this point in the series we have come to a stronghold that is unlike all the others in that it doesn't grow out of the ordinary interactions of people and events, but is constructed by points of direct contact with spiritual darkness. For some people this will be a lesson of little consequence—they have been blessed to have walked a path free and clear of trespassing into the occult domain. For others their immersion into the "depths of Satan" has been so devastating (whether of their own volition or forced upon them by others) that this chapter may seem like a pop gun, when what they need is a canon.[1]

For many of us, however, contact with this realm has been by dribs and drabs: A little here, a little there, and the infiltration into our lives through the generations before us may hardly have been noticed in its effects upon us. Indeed, this is a domain that prefers to remain hidden in that half-light where curious or spiritually hungry souls go to find "something more" in the way of spiritual life and experience—not necessarily wanting evil, but drawn towards things beyond the pale of orthodox Christian faith. By posing as legitimate spiritual experience the New Age has made huge inroads into Western culture. The spider knows how to make the web all but invisible to the unsuspecting fly it seeks to catch. The enemy is a deceiver! One pastor said deception is like falling asleep: You don't know you are asleep until someone tries to wake you.[2] Let spiritual darkness be exposed for what it is and we will all wake up and seek the safety and freedom our Lord offers.

The Occult Realm Identified in Scripture

The occult is an entry point for the enemy. Like trauma the occult can open doors for the enemy's kingdom to enter and oppress us, but unlike trauma we may not have been aware of anything obviously wrong in our times of contact with it.

Nevertheless, scripture shows that transgressing upon the occult is serious; in the Old Testament the penalty for it was death and no sacrifice could atone for it.[3] As New Testament believers we do not war against flesh and blood in this way, but Israel's example clearly shows us that we are not to be compromised by any involvement with the occult—we must keep it out of our lives.

The occult, like unforgiveness, is also a major block to healing. Until our contact with it is put under the Blood, it gives the enemy the legal right to bind and torment us with the curse of the law, since we let him lure us away from God's protection. The occult realm is a false god that seeks both worship (to become our heart's desire and daily focus) and service (to get us acting according to its desires). You don't have to love evil to worship and serve it; all you have to do is simply begin desiring the things it presents, thinking they are good. Then it's got your focus. Soon it gets you.

In ancient times, high places were sites where idol worship took place. Under our covenant prideful beliefs are the new high places where the Lord may be rejected in favor of that which is false.[4] This broad definition could apply in general to all of the operations of Satan's kingdom, but the occult, more narrowly and traditionally defined takes four main forms in scripture:

1) Worship of false gods (idol worship, false religions, cults)[5]

2) Forbidden ways of seeking knowledge of the future (astrology, fortune telling, prognostication)[6]

3) Forbidden contact with the dead (séances, mediums, Ouija)[7]

4) Forbidden ways of seeking to access spiritual power (witchcraft, sorcery, shamanism)[8]

The occult counterfeits genuine spiritual power and light (truth). In astronomy a planet that crosses in front of a star is said to cause an "occultation," meaning that the star is "hidden from view"—the dictionary definition of the occult.[9] This gives us a perfect picture of Satan's counterfeiting activity. Just as a planet reflects the sun's light, but has no fire of its own, so too the enemy seeks to draw our attention by a deceptive display of occult knowledge and power, while obscuring the wisdom and power that come through the One

True God and his servants.[10] Do not expect this kingdom to exhibit its dark side very often. Spiritual darkness prefers to disguise itself as light—at least in terms of attracting unsuspecting "flies" (us!) into its web. We would hardly walk into such a trap if we could see the evil on the other side.[11] This "occulting" activity of Satan is described in scripture. As you read these texts try to discern the false religion that spread around the world which began with the visitation of "an angel of light" to an unwary soul.[12]

And no wonder, for even Satan disguises himself as an angel of light. 2 Corinthians 11:14

But even if we or an angel from heaven should preach to you a gospel contrary to the one we preached to you, let him be accursed. Galatians 1:8

Temptations of the Occult

There are two main temptations of the occult. These are the "flesh hooks" that the tempter uses to snare the unwary.

1) Knowledge. The spirit behind it tempts with pride. Divination is the act or practice of trying to foretell the future by occult means. The cults also seek knowledge, claiming a superior and secret wisdom or way of salvation, but it doesn't come from God or the Bible.

2) Power. The spirit behind it tempts with control. Witchcraft and sorcery seek to make things happen by the power of the mind, special talents or natural elements. It is a form of control—a rebellion against God's order or authority.[13] Sorcery uses spells to control others or events; witchcraft uses objects. Both rely upon demons to do the real work.

Sorcery is a translation of the Greek word *pharmakia* used in Galatians 5:19 to describe one of the works of the flesh. This is the root for pharmaceuticals, our word for prescription drugs. There is a subtle caution here that dependency on prescription drugs can easily become a way of trying to bypass the curse of illness by not seeking to get right with God about what may be wrong in our hearts that is causing the physical problem (Chapter 1).[14]

Be alert to symptoms of occult penetration. The thoughts of the one being deceived become increasingly negative with an unhealthy interest in the "dark side" of life. The mind becomes confused, "foggy," blanks out easily, loses strength to think things through rationally and logically. Fear intensifies. A person is often bound to past occult contact in fear or pride. Other signs may include hatred of God, rejection of God's Word, inability to stay awake in church or when reading scripture.

The power of an occult experience to entrap people is built upon the temptation to believe in one's own experience and perspective above God's Word. Powerful deception comes from the way the occult spirits make the truth claims seem real. The connection is made by means of a subjective experience which conveys "authority" or credibility to the truth claim of the practice—whether it is a "spooky" feeling from ghosts in a house reputed to be haunted, or facts spoken during a séance that only the deceased could know, or crystal ball predictions that sometimes come true. If the final arbiter for the one becoming deceived is their own experience, *rather than the Bible*, the "spider's web" has not been set in vain. Like modern retailers, the enemy is a master at giving out "loss leaders," bits and pieces of knowledge or supernatural encounters, in order to get you to buy into what he wants to sell you. Then the real merchandising (the selling of your soul) begins. One occult activity, no matter how slight it seems, can easily lead into many other practices. Don't buy the lies! God desires that we choose life by avoiding that which He calls evil.[15]

Principles for Balanced Discernment

Keeping in mind C.S. Lewis' caution about becoming either too dismissive of or too obsessed with this realm (Chapter 4), we will want to have some sound principles of balance and discernment concerning occult contact. Consider the following for starters:

1) It is heart attachment to any wrong thing or habitual sin which evil spirits use to subvert our focus and cause us to perish—not the "flirtation" of momentary temptations.[16]

2) Agreement with any occult activity or belief opens doors. In terms of active transgression, it does not matter if we acted in innocence or deliberately. The lines are clearly drawn between the two kingdoms—any trespass is a very real transgression. Nevertheless, even as He holds us accountable, the Lord in His love for us looks upon the heart and may choose to cover with His protection what we have touched in ignorance.[17]

3) The devil is an extreme legalist and will seek to use any touching of the occult, any trespass into his territory, to activate the curse of the law—the negative consequences of our disobedience. It is wise to renounce all contact with the occult that you suspect you, or your past generations, may have made.[18]

4) Dependence upon any created thing is a form of idolatry. Are you hooked on it? Are you defending your involvement with unreasonable intensity?

5) There are "gray areas" of legitimate, honest disagreement among Christians about what is forbidden for us "to touch" because the scriptures are *suggestive* of application, but not always *definitive*. Paul's word in Corinthians on eating meat sacrificed to idols shows us a position of grace in a "gray area" of their day—leaving conviction to the individual's conscience about matters of possible legal defilement.[19]

6) The furthest reach of our liberty and God's covering grace are summed up in the phrase, "To the pure all things are pure." [20] However, we should always be willing to check the assumed purity of our motives. Just because we think something is harmless doesn't mean it is or that our reasons for being involved with it are aboveboard. Do not be deceived![21]

Time to Clean House

Sometimes it is necessary to do a house cleansing. Go through the rooms asking the Lord to show you if there are things that you have collected or were given to you that need to be cast out. Try not to become legalistic, but seek to discern with His help what dishonors the Lord you now serve. If it is clearly from the dark side, don't sell it to some poor unsuspecting soul—burn it or trash it. That's what the early church did.[22] While you are at it, do a house blessing. Go through the same rooms dedicating them to the Lord and welcoming His Spirit to fill your home with peace. Often people will make the sign of the cross over doors and other openings with oil or water that has been blessed by a simple prayer of consecration committing the oil or water to the Lord.

The Way to Freedom

Depending upon previous levels of involvement, gaining freedom from the occult can be simple or extremely laborious, especially if traumatic events took place. These steps are for light to moderate involvement with occult activities. Every chapter in the book will be needed where more severe penetration occurred.

1) Recognize, repent and renounce any involvement in occult activities by family members or ancestors, putting it under the Blood of Christ and breaking the curse in Jesus' Name.

2) Take full responsibility for any contact or involvement with occult activities you may have had: Repent, renounce in the same manner, carrying every activity captive to Christ.

3) Turn to the Father and release gratitude that there are no sins and no powers on earth that can separate you from His love!

Father, thank You that You have both the power and the loving desire to cleanse me from all occult contact. Jesus, thank You for the Blood that You shed which is my liberation and the enemy's doom. Holy Spirit, thank You for leading me into all truth by removing the veil of deception that blinded me in the past. I ask for and gratefully receive all of Your ministry to me in this area. Please continue in every way to lead me out of darkness into Your glorious Kingdom of Light! I renounce any occult practices in the generations of my fathers and I repent of having walked in them myself. I repent of my own involvement or contact with _____. Forgive me and break its power over me and my generations. Wash me with the Blood of Christ. Fill me and seal me with Your Spirit.

CHAPTER 21

FEAR NOT!

The Stronghold of Fear

What are you afraid of? OK, maybe you aren't afraid of anything. Let's put it this way: Are you anxious, do you experience dread over certain events, are you weighted down with concerns, are you chronically worried, stressed out, or shy around people? Like so many others, perhaps you avoid speaking in public, or want to run from times of conflict and confrontation? All these are forms of fear! As such they stand in the way of the life Jesus wants to live in us. Jesus is the Fearless One who has overcome the world, the flesh, and the devil, and is bringing to us the perfect love of the Father so that we too can become overcoming ones and live valiant lives, trusting our God even in situations of great peril.

Fear is therefore a mighty stronghold that the enemy seeks to build in every believer to quench faith, stymie love and turn us away from the challenges of our high calling. Fear is built upon the other strongholds we have been studying: unbelief in God's perfect love is the root to all fears; accusation makes us feel cut off and condemned; bitterness binds the pain of the past to us; unhealed trauma makes our world feel very insecure; rejection sends frightful messages to our heart; self-rejection blocks us from believing that God really can love us; envy insists that others are getting a better deal; and occult involvement always brings massive amounts of fear. No wonder that fear is something of an emotional pandemic! Fortunately for all of us, the Lord has great remedies!

Two Forms of Legitimate Fear

There are two kinds of fear that are good and helpful: godly fear and fear awareness of immediate danger. Even so, we need to beware—both of these can quickly turn into the wrong kind of fear.

1) Godly fear is respect, honor and acknowledgment of who God is. It is a healthy awareness that God holds us accountable for our choices. On the other hand, being afraid of God, or of

what God may do, or of what God may allow, or of what God may ask of us comes from the enemy.

2) Fear awareness of immediate danger enables us to deal with trouble and rescue the situation. Science has identified this as the "flight or fight" response of the General Adaptation Syndrome (review Chapter 1) and we need it to gear our bodies up for immediate action. This can quickly become "bad fear" if a) we are paralyzed or panicked and cannot act decisively or b) there is no real response we can make because we are being alarmed by imagined or future dangers, not immediate, life-threatening ones. This kind of fear response keeps most people living stressed up and breaks down health like a hammer.

Apart from these good types of fear, all other forms are due to not trusting God. The critical issue is heart-trust in God.

You keep him in perfect peace whose mind is stayed on you, because he trusts in you. Trust in the Lord forever, for the Lord God is an everlasting rock. Isaiah 26:3-4

An Anatomy of Fear

If you want freedom you need to know that fear is a spiritual issue—not a personality problem. Watch this progression carefully. It will help you recognize and renounce any agreements with fear you may have. Remember, the enemy tempts us with very persuasive ideas, images and impressions. Stand on God's truth!

1) Fear is the opposite of love. Just as perfect love casts out fear, so too "perfect fear" casts out love. Fear closes us in on Self (our old nemesis), activating selfishness, self-centeredness and above all self-protectiveness. Faith and trust open us, enabling us to care for others in the self-less way of love.[1]

2) Fear is weakened faith. Jesus upbraided the disciples for having "little faith" and "no faith" when they became worried about their daily needs and afraid during the storm at sea.[2] Such concerns *seem* normal, but Jesus shows us that it is "illegal" for a follower of His to fall into fear in any of its forms.

3) Fear is the opposite of faith. Fear works in the same way faith does but in the opposite direction. Faith looks past the problem of the visible reality to see its solution in the invisible reality of God and therefore becomes the substance in us that God uses to fulfill His purposes.[3] Fear looks at the visible problem, ignores the invisible Savior, and becomes the substance the enemy uses to fulfill his plans for us. Job lamented that what he feared came upon him.[4] It is false "protection" that works against us.

4) Fear is spiritual blindness. It keeps us from seeing with our eyes of faith. It minimizes what God can do, "shrinks" us as His vessels and "giganticizes" the problem.[5]

5) Fear is actually a sin. Fear is distrust in God, rooted in the sin of unbelief, for whatever is not of faith/trust in God is sin.[6]

6) Fear is spiritual bondage. It enslaves us and carries us captive to the enemy's mindset, pressuring us to act amiss.[7]

7) Fear is an evil spirit. It delights in using fear to derail our life and destroy our health. These spirits are liars and bullies who never tell you *the whole truth*—otherwise you would quickly go back to trusting God as you were before they showed up.

As Paul wrote to timid Timothy, it was not God who gave us "a spirit of fear." What God gives us is "power, love and a sound mind."[8] Note that we have a choice to make: We can have either fear *or* power, love and a sound mind. We cannot have it both ways! Even the presence of a little stress can begin robbing anyone of confidence in God, feelings of love and soundness of mind (thinking clearly, remembering readily). On the other hand, reconnect your faith with confidence in God's power, love and wisdom and see how quickly fear is sent packing.

Finding Freedom from Fear

There are many effective ways of getting free from the power of fear—try these out in addition to the steps of Chapter 7.[9]

1) Receive: Let perfect love cast out fear.[10] Work on renewing the true image of God in your heart, keeping your thoughts fixed on

Him.[11] Meditate upon His love expressed for you at the cross.[12] Open your heart and receive His love by faith.

2) Believe: God's Word undercuts the power of fear, so build your faith by staying in the Word.[13] *Saying* scripture over and over has power to slowly push back the attack of fear. *Believing* scripture has awesome and immediate power once it becomes a living and life-giving Word to you. Take your stand on the truth as Jesus did. Stoutly resist the temptation to fear.

3) Resist: Keep obeying despite your fears! Refuse to let fear push you around, shut you down, or stop you.[14] Taking decisive action ("just *do* it") defeats a lot of fears during the trial and those same fears will have less power over you in future trials.

4) Rebuke: Prayers of command can cast out fear. Call a friend who can do spiritual warfare to break fear's grip on you.

5) Love: Whenever love fills our heart, fear becomes an out-cast. Start with friendly animals; work up to friendly people.

6) Rejoice: Laughter releases the grip of fear.[15]

7) Surrender: A willingness to suffer, even die, for Christ defeats most fears, since the fear of death is the root of all fears.[16] When we "die to Self," not caring what happens so long as His good will is done, we slip out of the snare of many fears.[17] The overcomers of Revelation 12:11 "loved not their own lives" even in the face of death. Surrender always brings peace and release.

8) Pray: Put your fears to rest as you release your concerns to God. Cast your cares on Him by praying concerns out of your heart and into His Hands, persevering until you let it all go.[18]

9) Discern: Learn to recognize the voice of fear (the way it presses upon you) and stop listening to it.[19]

An Ongoing Battle

Oddly enough the best time to start trusting God is when you are caught in fear. Jesus used a storm-tossed and windswept sea to offer His first "class" in walking on water.[20] He waited for fear to strike His disciples *before* challenging them to trust Him. The

Psalmist would have approved. Note that the repeated use of "will" indicates a deliberate choice.

When I am afraid, I will put my trust in you… In God I put my trust. I will not be afraid. What can flesh do to me? Psalm 56:3-4 WEB

The very best way to get free of persistent fear is by the six steps to freedom laid out for you in Chapter 7. Along the way to victory you will "see" a threefold progression: Faith becomes seeing; seeing becomes believing; believing becomes resting in confidence.

1) Jesus has overcome the world—He will always be victorious. This is the "seeing stage" as faith opens our eyes to see Jesus as the answer because of what He has done and can do.

"In the world you will have tribulation. But take heart; I have overcome the world." John 16:33

2) We overcome through faith in Him, not through faith in ourselves. Our faith in God's love and power is what overpowers our fear—one battle at a time. This is the "believing stage": We work hard at believing that what we see in Him is true.

For everyone who has been born of God overcomes the world. And this is the victory that has overcome the world—our faith. 1 John 5:4

3) Our heart becomes established as we make progress at more continually beholding God's perfect love for us and His power to give us victories. This is the "resting stage": We trust Him enough to stay centered and surrendered most of the time.

There is no fear in love, but perfect love casts out fear. For fear has to do with punishment. 1 John 4:18

Faith lifts and leads; fear presses and prods. Fear focuses on the thing feared—never on God. Learn to recognize when you are in fear and deal with it first—then you will be able to work with the problem it represents and receive the Lord's guidance and help much more readily. Ask the fruitful question: "What am I really afraid of?" Find it and deal with it! It is actually an act of faithfullness to confess our fears as unbelief and sin. Our Father loves an honest conversation, even if it is about our failings. Naming fear as sin begins the process of repentance and restoration to trust. As we do this we enter into fellowship with the Father about the truth of our situation. The problem is not with God—in what He has allowed—it is with our inability or unwillingness to trust Him with it. Now that we are talking it over with Him, we can draw strength from our relationship. So let us go boldly to the throne of grace and obtain mercy, then re-discover that His grace really is sufficient to help us in our time of need.[21]

The Way to Freedom

Some fears are easy to see; others are much harder to recognize—we have lived with them for so long that they seem normal and natural: "Of course I'm stressed, look at my situation!" The key is to focus on recovering the lost trust in God.

1) Be willing to recognize *any loss of peace* and any advent of stress as temptations coming from a spirit of fear—unless some other negative emotion is clearly predominating (such as anger).

2) Take full responsibility for agreeing with fear, losing peace and becoming "stressed": Repent, renounce and carry it captive to Christ until you see something in Him that restores trust.

3) Turn to the Father and release gratitude to Him that His perfect love is always able to cast out your fear!

Father, forgive me for falling into fear again. Thank You that I can come boldly into Your Presence and ask You to cleanse me of this sin. Thank You that You love me and want to fellowship with me even now. Thank You that You have made great plans for how to help me and that even this situation will be made to work for my good. I ask You to send Jesus for my deliverance and to meet me by Your Spirit right where I am, as I am, and lead me forward. Strengthen me to hold on to You as I resist fear and watch for Your final victory to arrive.

CHAPTER 22

NO MORE IDOLS!

The Stronghold of Addiction

In the previous chapters on strongholds we examined each one in its uniqueness. With this lesson we will explore the common elements that constitute their binding power. Although this is a lesson focused upon addictions, it actually applies to anything in life that we can't "just say no" to. That is because the ground beneath the cross is level. People with addictions are not a special class of sinners. All of us have been badly broken by the Fall and need to be saved and mended by the love and mercy of God. The root issues are the same for all of us. The path of redemption and restoration is also the same: We are all saved *by grace through faith.*

For by grace you have been saved through faith. And this is not your own doing; it is the gift of God. Ephesians 2:8

Understanding Addictions

Narrowly defined addictions have to do with substance abuse; a wider term for addictions, one that is Biblical, is *a besetting sin*. The besetting sin is the sin that "besets" us—assails us and hems us in—whenever the temptation for it comes along. Certainly this scripture applies to those who are beset with substance abuse issues, but it applies equally well to those who can't seem to give up being judgmental or jealous or worried. Carefully study this passage from Hebrews. These are deeply instructive of our freedom. For instance, when you are Hungry, Angry, Lonely or Tired, it is time to H.A.L.T.—lay aside that weight, then get your focus back before trying to go on. Where should our focus be? On the Lord. Looking to Him we prevail!

Wherefore <u>seeing we also are compassed about</u> with so great a cloud of witnesses, let us <u>lay aside every weight</u>, and the sin which doth so easily beset us, and let us <u>run with patience</u> the race that is set before us, <u>looking unto Jesus</u> the author and finisher of our faith; who for the joy that was set before him <u>endured the cross</u>, despising the

shame, and is set down at the right hand of the throne of God.
Hebrews 12:1-2 KJV

What is an addiction? An addiction is anything that controls us and holds us in bondage. That which controls us, rules us, and whenever it gets triggered, God is not our master—sin is.[1] Whatever we cannot just say no to (that which is not of God) holds us in its power. It seeks to enslave us,[2] then destroy us and in the process, destroy as many others as it can.[3] Some things that are good can become an addiction when moderation is exceeded. Some things are no good to begin with. There are many forms that addictions can take:

Legal and illegal drugs	Alcohol	Eating disorders
Foul language	Sexual sins	Pornography
Relationships	"Workaholism"	Gambling
Shopping	Entertainment	Compulsive behaviors
The love of money	Obsessions	Worry, anxiety, panic

Combating Addictions

Learn the "want to want to" prayer: "Lord, help me want to want what You want and hate what You hate." This enlists the Lord to work with your emotional life and honestly admits to God that deep down *in this moment* a large part of you doesn't want His will. Like Esau you are being strongly tempted to trade your inheritance for a bowl of porridge.[4] Remember the teaching on who we are in Christ (Chapter 9)? No matter how much we may crave the wrong thing, that desire is still not who we really are now as New Creations. The real you truly does want what He wants. The real you already has the nature of Jesus joined to you by the Spirit. Even so, all you may "see" of the new you is a tiny wish that you weren't so weak against the temptation. That's the "David" in you wanting to take down your "Goliath" side. Don't get in his way!

The number one way of escape is running to God.[5] Many run *from* God, instead of *to* God. Many run from their troubles, their weaknesses, their failings, rather than face them, winding up in even worse predicaments. Hear this life-saving promise: We are absolutely, unconditionally promised that *everyone* who calls on the Name of the Lord *will* be saved (rescued, delivered, restored).

The same Lord is Lord of all, bestowing his riches on all who call on him. For "<u>everyone</u> who calls on the name of the Lord <u>will</u> be saved." Romans 10:12-13

To get free of any besetting sin we have to learn to call and keep on calling on the Lord—learning how to lean hard on Him and draw on His saving help, casting *all* our hope on Him and hanging on for dear life. How much do you have to call? As much as it takes, as often as it takes, as long as it takes. Our full recovery requires becoming 100% surrendered to and committed to God. There is no peace, no victory without surrender. We cannot be 90% surrendered to the Lord and still gain lasting victory over any besetting sin. Since we will never be more committed to God than we believe *deep down* that God is committed to us, believing the truth about our Father's love is truly a life and death issue. It was for Jesus—He was willing to die to reveal the Father to us.[6] Believing the truth about your Father's unflinching and amazing love for you is the cure for backsliding—once it is believed in enough for you to run to Him, rather than from Him.

Three Powerful Lies

Three deadly deceptions of the enemy have tremendous binding power.[7] These lies must be recognized and cast down.

Lie #1) The Lie of the Idol: The spirit behind the idol promises to give life to those it seeks to capture. The strong grip of addiction upon the soon-to-be enslaved one comes from a spiritual power working through the idol to steal, kill or destroy. Remember that an idol is anything that we place *above* God, anything that we want *more* than God.

What am I saying then? That a thing sacrificed to idols is anything, or that an idol is anything? But I say that the things which the Gentiles sacrifice, they sacrifice to demons, and not to God, and I don't desire that you would have communion with demons. 1 Corinthians 10:20 WEB

Demons still offer a "fix" in exchange for worship. Worship means "to ascribe worth to." It also translates as "to serve." How have you been serving them? What are they saying to you? Does it sound anything like this?

> *Come to me and I will give you power to mend your life. Give yourself to me and I will satisfy you. I will ease the pain and give you gain.*

Lie #2) The Lie of the Wounded Heart: This keeps the one bound looking in the wrong direction, but the problem is not "out there" (in the world of things to get or people to blame) and can't be fixed out there. The problem lies within—in a heart so broken that it desperately needs a great love to heal it. The root cause of addiction is pain where love should have been. It has been famously observed that "the young man who rings the bell at the brothel is unconsciously looking for God."[8] All such attempts to fill the "God void" the wrong way are doomed to failure, often resulting in bondage. Being disgusted with one's self over the besetting sin doesn't help; it actually increases sin's bondage through self-hatred and self-rejection (Chapter 18).

Lie #3) The Lie of the Distorted Image: Only the revelation of the Father's great love can mend such a broken heart, but a distorted image of the Father keeps the one bound running *from* God, rather than *to* Him—the root cause of backsliding. A distorted image of self binds the pain of self-rejection in the heart (Chapters 8-10). Both images need thorough cleansing and mending in order to liberate the heart from these deep roots of the besetting sin.

Satan is a liar from the beginning. His lies are very convincing and once they have had a chance to impact our feeling system, they become powerful strongholds within us. Our task is to recognize and renounce those lies, carry them captive to Christ and then come into agreement with God's truths.[9] This is war so be prepared to go to battle stations at a moment's notice. Don't tarry in the pig pen like the prodigal did—race to your Father at the first sign of weakness. Take that Hebrews 4:16 "elevator" straight to His throne of grace. As quickly as you can, obtain the mercy and find the grace

He so freely wants to give you. The great thing is not walking perfectly, so that you never stumble over bumps in the road, but learning to recover quickly before falling on your face.

We are clearly instructed that we are saved by grace through faith.[10] Therefore, in order to overcome our besetting sins, compulsions and addictions we will need to grow a great faith in the greatness of the saving grace of God:

1) We will need to call on the Name of the Lord for rescue.[11]

2) We will need a "love of the truth that we may be saved"—so that we will stay determined to fight to the death against believing the three lies in our moments of doubt and pain.[12]

3) We will need balance concerning our struggle with the flesh. At times we can simply "rest in the Lord," trusting that the flesh has been "crucified for us" and that His work in us will prevail.[13] At other times we must be prepared to "crucify the flesh" ourselves, praying and persevering against the stronghold as if it all depends upon us.[14]

4) We will need wisdom in discerning when to fight and how to trust: Under attack we fight as if it all depends on us, yet trust *even then* that our victory depends entirely upon Him.[15]

4) We will need a willingness to fight to the death. Depending upon the power of the stronghold that has grown in us from habitual past sins, we will need a holy resolve and determination to choose to die fighting for our freedom (if it comes to that), rather than give in to the old bondage and become slaves to sin again (Luke 9:23-25; Revelation 12:11).

> **Consider him who endured from sinners such hostility against himself, so that you may not grow weary or fainthearted. In your struggle against sin you have not yet resisted to the point of shedding your blood.** Hebrews 12:3-4

If you find yourself in a season of protracted struggle and fierce temptation, don't let your trial be wasted! Don't try to get out of your trials so quickly that you don't take the time to look up to the Father and make sure your heart believes that even while you are "at your worst," even when your weaknesses are in your face, even when you seem filled with wrong desire or shameful emotions, *even in those moments* He is loving you, covering you with immense mercy and grace, cheering for you, and desiring your conversation and fellowship—over the sins or temptations you are struggling with! Get a good look by faith at the beautiful, grace-giving God who loves us even in our places of disgrace. This breaks the deep grip of shame over our fallenness that came in through Adam's nature. But don't try to feel these things, just refresh your heart by saying to Him what His Word says is true about Him.

The Way to Freedom

The self-blinding barrier of denial must be broken through before any addiction can be recognized for what it is and honestly resisted. Assuming that has already happened, then the following steps can be doggedly pursued. Victory rarely comes easily.

1) Take full responsibility for every aspect of the addiction you have recognized: Repent, renounce making it an idol you worshiped and served so whole-heartedly.

2) Carry every area of disobedience and rebellion captive to Christ until you see something in Him that restores your trust and confidence in God's love and mercy for you and His power to help you.

3) Turn to the Father and release gratitude to Him that even in your worst places of disgrace He covers you with His grace! Pray for a passion to worship and serve Him instead of the idol.

4) Be prepared to call on His Name at a moment's notice!

Father, thank You that You are loving me with perfect, unconditional love even now, even in times of great trial and temptation. You are not holding my weaknesses against me. What an amazing God you are! Your gentleness is making me great and giving me strength. Your strength is even now being made perfect in my weakness! Your perfect love is casting out my fears! You are at work even through this for my good. I am truly finding Your grace in my place of dis-grace! Keep coming to my rescue as I call on Your Name.

SECTION FOUR:
THE JOURNEY FORWARD

"How narrow is the gate,
and restricted is the way that leads to life!
Few are those who find it."
Matthew 7:14 WEB

CHAPTER 23

SPIRITUAL WARFARE 101

The New Stronghold of Surrender

Now that we have worked our way through the many strongholds that typically afflict and hinder our life in Christ, these lessons could seem overwhelming. "It's too complicated!" is the legitimate cry of a heart yearning for freedom as well as transformation. We surely need a principle of simplicity or we may quickly fall again into bondage. Jesus said, "How narrow is the gate and restricted is the way that leads to life."[1] His way seems "restricted" at times, but it is always simple. Children live in the Kingdom far better than we do.[2] The really hard part is re-learning how to stay surrendered to the Giver of Life, something we could all do as children. An old hymn summarizes the walk nicely: "Trust and obey for there's no other way to be happy in Jesus, but to trust and obey."[3] This chapter is about the warfare around trusting (the "narrow gate"); the next chapter will be about guidance—learning to walk in the sometimes "difficult way" of obedience to the Spirit.

Our Number One Assignment

Spiritual Warfare 101 points us to the elementary battle of our daily life in Christ. Our job as "soldiers" is to make sure that our hearts stay surrendered to the Lord throughout the day—keeping us willing and able to trust and obey our Master and Commander (who is also our best Friend). This is our number one assignment in life given to us by Jesus Himself as the "first and great" commandment.[4] Loving God with our whole hearts certainly entails giving the whole of our life over to Him in full submission to His leadership. Such surrender and centering of our life in Him is not possible without the gift of faith; living un-surrendered and un-centered in Him is unthinkable once true faith has come. Indeed a *living faith* always carries us into this position of humble, trusting dependence and willingness to follow the One who has revealed such love to us.[5]

Either our hearts are moving towards surrender or they are drifting into the Great Rebellion. This not Star Trek: There is no Neutral Zone. There are only two spiritual principles at work in our universe and they are *always* at work upon us. This is why the keeping of the first commandment is so critical to our life mission: We cannot fulfill our secondary purpose in the lives of others if we do not learn to stay united to His life (our primary purpose). The level of peace and confidence we have in God will declare the issue all day long—that's God's way of giving us feedback moment by moment on how well we are doing with the most important thing we need to be doing—trusting and obeying Him.[6] This is the battle for one's own life—and it is waged in the heart.[7]

In boot camp all new recruits are issued rifles and taught to protect their lives and the lives of their comrades. In the "battle" of daily life our rifle is our heart! The enemy wants to get his finger on the trigger of our heart and start firing it off at ourselves and others. Such "misfires" are almost irresistible when we don't keep our heart clean and clear in the Lord (of negative emotions and stronghold issues). But suppose the Lord gets His finger on your heart, then He can use you to give mercy, peace and patience where it is needed as you go through your day. That's much better isn't it? So our heart is a powerful weapon for advancing either the Kingdom of God or the kingdom of darkness.

Trusting His Hands; Seeking His Face

Here is another principle of simplicity that companions with trust and obey: No matter what the enemy is doing, God is also at work to accomplish His good purposes. This is especially true of the dynamics of transformation. Since the great battle of daily life is for our heart, we need to trust His Hands and seek His Face.

1) His Hands: God is at work on *all things* in our lives with one great purpose in mind. We need to know, understand and be in agreement with that purpose, or our lives will not make sense, nor will we realize the focal point of the enemy's attacks. God's Hands are always at work to conform you to Christ—shaping you *from the outside in*. Picture the Lord reaching through all of

the outward circumstances of your life, seeking to "center you" on the Potter's Wheel.[8] What is His goal in each and every moment? To draw out of you a Christlike response, or (if you can't yet do that) to prepare you to be able to respond as the New Creation you are at some point down the road. The ultimate good that God has in mind is not just His blessings being poured into our lives, but the incomparable blessing of actually becoming more like Jesus in all of our ways *in this life*.

> And we know that for those who love God <u>all things</u> work together for good, for those who are called according to his purpose. For those whom he foreknew he also predestined to be <u>conformed</u> to the image of his Son. Romans 8:28-29

2) His Face: What is God's work on our interior? His primary purpose is to transform us into the Image of His Son *from the inside out*—by revealing His Image to us. The Father reveals the Son; the Son reveals the Father.[9] Whenever we get our spiritual eyes back on Jesus, we experience a shift from being self-centered to being Christ-centered. This interior transformation happens as we "see" by faith some offering of grace in Jesus that enables us to fully surrender to whatever He has allowed or is asking of us in His sovereignty. Once we again become centered and surrendered, submitted and committed, the good fruit of His Spirit flows into us and through us. In this way His Face transforms us into His Image (Chapter 8).[10]

> But we all, with unveiled face beholding as in a mirror the glory of the Lord, are <u>transformed</u> into the same image from glory to glory, even as from the Lord, the Spirit. 2 Corinthians 3:18 WEB

These two great works of God are going on all of the time. Always the Father's Hands are upon us to raise up whatever we surrender to Him and to work through all things to increase our willingness to surrender all, even if we are fighting against what He is doing through our ignorance of His ways. At the same time the revelation of Jesus Christ is working within us at all times, however little we may be aware of it, to transform the way that we live and to enable us to surrender to the Father. But *this process can be greatly enhanced by our cooperation*. We can make it our goal to more frequently choose to surrender to the work of His Hands; we can also choose to more actively seek His Face and re-surrender at any moment. As you learn this you will discover that you are in the "driver's seat" where your spiritual growth is concerned!

Let's see how this plays out. The Father has His hands on our lives like a Master Potter working with absolutely everything (the good, the bad and the seemingly indifferent) to accomplish His great desire—to refashion us into children who display the nature of His Son. As a potter exerts great pressure with his hands to center clay on the wheel, the Father also works through the stress in our lives to bring us again and again to the place of inward surrender. Like un-centered clay we often try to fly off the wheel! But under the pressure ("humble yourselves under the mighty hand...")[11] we finally stretch our faith vision to see something in the Lord that helps us to yield our stubborn resistance and say, "Not my will, but Yours be done." *The work of His hands helps us to seek His Face!* From this hallowed place of surrender the Father is able to raise us into new life—just as a potter raises the centered clay into the form he envisions.[12]

Going through Our Day like Jesus

Since the Father is working 24/7 to conform us to Christ, it will certainly help us to cooperate with Him if we gain vision for what that looks like. Though outward works are important fruit to cultivate, for the purpose of this series, let's consider what it means to be conformed to Christ in terms of the inner life and your emotional state.[13] Would you like to go through your days the way Jesus did? No one alive has walked through daily life with more love, more peace, or more joy. Yet no one alive has ever had a tougher assignment to carry out or faced more opposition. Consider how your approach to daily life might change if you would follow Jesus in these ways:

1) Love and joy: Jesus was able to keep joy and love alive in His Heart because He was masterful at forgiving sinful people. Would you like to go through your day free of hurt and offense *like Jesus did*? You have Him inside of you to help you forgive.

2) Acceptance: Jesus suffered rejection by many people He deeply loved, yet He was able to live with His Heart secure, knowing He was loved by the One who matters most. Would you like to go through your day protected and filled by God's love for you *like Jesus did*? You have the same Father devoted to you. Value His acceptance of you above other's opinions.

3) Peace and guidance: Jesus was able to live in complete dependence upon God's control of the world, not His, and yet He was peace-filled all of the time, no matter what the enemy was stirring up, because He kept trusting the Father *with* all things and was willing to obey *in* all things. Would you like to go through your day with peace and trust *like Jesus did*? You have a new nature in you that loves to live His way.

4) Stress free: Jesus saw people all around Him carrying heavy burdens and living with great anguish and injustice, but He never got burned out, over-burdened, angry or depressed in serving God. Would you like to be able to care for others in your daily life *like Jesus did*? He is right beside you, willing to help you learn how to let Him carry your burdens.

This is the way of life that Jesus wants to live in us by His Spirit, and our Father is so zealous for giving it to us that He is making *all things* serve this higher purpose. What's to stop us?

The Counter Feints of the Enemy

Certainly the enemy cannot stop this work of the Father's Hands —he is a defeated foe! God hates every evil and has determined and declared that *all things* will be made to work for the good of the people He is redeeming. Meditate on this life-changing truth: *The enemy cannot make the evil he does through human sin stick to anyone.* God will overturn it all and make even the worst things the enemy does work for our good. So how does the enemy make evil stick? By getting us to bind the hurt, pain and injustice of the past to ourselves through bitterness of heart and by unbelief in God's promises. We are being manipulated into becoming our own captors! This is monstrous, outrageous and infernally ingenious all at the same time. Don't fall for it a moment longer!

If God is working *upon us* through all things by His hands and working *within us* through all things by His Spirit to conform us to Christ, then the enemy (having read the Bible) is also working through everything to oppose God's work by a) tempting us to doubt that all things are working for our good (thus trying to counter the work of His hands) and b) by "drawing us away" from the revelation of Jesus Christ (thus trying to counter the work of His Face).[14] As Dr. Jack Deere once said, "The enemy has W.M.D.'s of his own—Weapons of Mass Distraction."[15]

Once we are no longer beholding our God with a heart of confident faith, we are prey to the enemy and of little threat to his kingdom. Even worse, we are unwittingly being re-shaped into the image of the ultimate fallen one, Satan, who is the most un-forgiving and anxious being in the universe. Have you been tempted to doubt the work of God's Hands? Have you been distracted from keeping your focus on Jesus? Then be prepared to fight! You get to choose what you want to believe and whose image you want to focus on and live by. If something in you doesn't want to trust in, surrender to and rely upon your God you have just met the enemy's handiwork—don't let it reign over you. Carry it captive to Christ instead. Like those who rebuilt the walls of Jerusalem, we have to learn to do the work of the Kingdom with our sword and shield at our side if we want to see the old stronghold walls of self-protection come down and the new, glorious walls of His salvation go up.[16] How long will that campaign take? Only He knows. But we can be sure of this: It will be well worth the effort it takes to fully enter His Kingdom in this life. Fight the good fight of faith![17]

Father, thank You for all of the ways that You are training me for those conflicts with the enemy that cannot be avoided. May I ever trust that You are also fighting with me and for me. I fully accept this calling upon my life—to fight the good fight of faith—and I realize that the first battle is always for my own heart—to keep it surrendered to You. Make me willing to be made willing to surrender everything to You, each and every day.

CHAPTER 24

WALKING IN THE SPIRIT

The New Stronghold of Submission

It would hardly be fair or right, having given so much attention to the enemy's ways of distracting us, mis-leading us, and hindering us with strongholds, to finish this series without giving time to the Lord and His ways of leading us in new life. After all, the point is not to pull the emotional strongholds down (either of the past or of the present) just so that we can be free of them—as good as that is. Rather, our quest is to become free so that we can *now* follow Jesus in everything! The truly healed and restored life is one that is continually given over to the Lord, seeking to walk with Him as He leads the way. For that we will need to learn how to "walk in the Spirit" that He supplies.[1]

Let us begin by acknowledging that as great as His Word is—He even set it above His Name—God speaks to us in many more ways than scripture alone.[2] We are guided by His example (Jesus' life is a *visible* word—a word *shown* to us), His voice (a word *spoken* to us, however we may receive it), and His Spirit (a word *living* in us, however He may inspire us). It is easy to see from this that there is a progression of increasing intimacy from following the written Word of scripture to imitating Jesus' example to listening for His voice to yielding the whole flow of our daily life to His Spirit. Jesus gave us—His Bride on earth—more than a book when He pledged Himself to us as our Husband. He gave *Himself* to us![3]

Our new life in Christ comes through the forgiveness of our sins and through the gift of the indwelling Holy Spirit.[4] Just as Jesus *died our death for us*, so now He desires to *live His life in us* and through us. This happens beautifully whenever we yield ourselves to the Holy Spirit and walk in the steps He shows us. Whenever we are released to trust and obey, Jesus "comes to life" in us!

I have been crucified with Christ [in Him I have shared His crucifixion]; **it is no longer I who live, but Christ (the Messiah) lives in me; and the life I now live in the body I live by faith in (by adherence to and reliance on and complete trust in) the Son of God, Who loved me and gave Himself up for me.** Galatians 2:20 AMP

Walking in the Spirit has two distinct dimensions: conscious and unconscious. Though this may be a strange way of phrasing it, the truth is that we have been "sleep walking" with the Lord all of our lives. That is, He has been guiding us in countless ways all along, but we may not have been consciously aware of the many specific ways by which He has done so. Our first task, therefore, is to identify and understand these hidden ways of *un-self-conscious* guidance. The Holy Spirit is like the perfect waiter who doesn't intrude upon our privacy by making His ways of serving us obvious. It is up to us to learn how to acknowledge Him so that He can more intimately and overtly direct our paths.

> **Lean on, trust in,** *and* **be confident in the Lord with all your heart** *and* **mind and do not rely on your own insight** *or* **understanding. In all your ways know, recognize,** *and* **acknowledge Him, and He will direct** *and* **make straight** *and* **plain your paths.** Proverbs 3:5-6 AMP

Dimension One: Unselfconscious Guidance

Walking in the Spirit is like breathing which is hardly surprising since He is called the "breath of the Almighty" and He is the "breath" of life imparted to us both in creation and in the new birth.[5] This Spirit-empowered walk, therefore, is easy and natural—literally child's play! In fact it was the Spirit, the great Teacher and Giver of life, who "secretly" taught us how to suckle, to eat, to speak, to walk, even to play. Every good thing about us including childhood is His gift to us, or will we have some "work" of our own apart from God to boast about? Not according to scripture, which says that we are saved by grace through faith and that not of ourselves, *not of our works,* "lest anyone should boast."[6] So let us acknowledge then that this Spirit-empowered walk has been going on since birth *as His gift to us.* God said that even the "infancy" of Israel, the forty years of their wilderness journey, was a time when He "carried Israel" as a child: He led them through it all and then explained it to them later, so that they could understand and acknowledge what He had done.[7]

158

And in the wilderness, where you have seen how the Lord your God carried you, as a man carries his son, all the way that you went until you came to this place. Deuteronomy 1:31

To this day the greatest exemplars of what it is like to walk in the Spirit and display the fruit of the Spirit are little children.[8] Their sparkling qualities are His gift of grace to them and through them to us! Children are simply more open and trusting than we are, which makes them such splendid receivers of grace that they are masters at living in the Kingdom, showing us the way to go.[9]

But Jesus called them to him, saying, "Let the children come to me, and do not hinder them, for to such belongs the kingdom of God. Truly, I say to you, whoever does not receive the kingdom of God like a child shall not enter it." Luke 18:16-17

The Holy Spirit has been with us all along. He is always teaching us and leading us into life. He is the Giver and Sustainer of life.[10] Jesus told His disciples *before* the events of Easter and Pentecost that they already "knew" the Holy Spirit He would be sending because the Spirit had been dwelling "with" them and would soon be "in" them.[11] This same Spirit has been unceasingly with you in your journey, helping you, guiding you, teaching you and comforting you, even before you became a Christian, even from before birth![12]

Now the word of the Lord came to me, saying, "Before I formed you in the womb I knew you, and before you were born I consecrated you; I appointed you a prophet to the nations." Jeremiah 1:4-5

St. Augustine put it this way: "Love God and do as you please."[13] He means of course that once we "love God" by surrendering to Him everything about our lives and loved ones and are willing to do His will above our own, *then* He begins to draw us by desires that please Him as well as ourselves. Only fully yielded Christians can live the way Augustine recommends. However, even before we knew Him, God was already drawing us into doing many things that pleased us as well as Him. Examples of this are eating, sleeping, befriending, parenting, working, loving and laughing.[14] No one needs conscious guidance from the Lord to do good things which come to us with such natural grace attached.

> [Not in your own strength] **for it is God Who is all the while effectually at work in you** [energizing and creating in you the power and desire], **both to will and to work for His good pleasure** *and* **satisfaction** *and* **delight.** Philippians 2:13 AMP

Trusting is, therefore, essential to these everyday ways of Spirit-empowered guidance, since any interference by negative emotions disturbs the childlike manner of our walk. Proverbs calls us to acknowledge Him and *trust* Him, that He may "direct our paths."[15] Guidance happens naturally for trusting hearts as Hannah Whitall Smith explains in *The Christian's Secret of a Happy Life.*[16]

> Above everything else trust Him... God cannot guide those souls who never trust Him enough to believe that He is doing it.

Dimension Two: Christ-Conscious Guidance

The Spirit-empowered walk described above is childlike and free. Not even being aware that it is happening is *almost* one of its requirements! On the other hand, the Spirit-led walk actually does require conscious and conscientious diligence and care in seeking it. It is harder work at first, but it is the way of the wise.[17] The first principle of seeking this kind of "awake and aware" guidance is: "Don't ask, if you don't really want to know." The Lord is not out to satisfy our intellectual *curiosity* about His will! He is interested in leading us through our *obedience* to His will. The likelihood exists that He may not tell you what you want to hear, so be prepared to yield to His will and avoid the pitfall of poor King Ahab who didn't want his plans disturbed by a contrary word from the Lord.[18] As Hannah Whitall Smith advises, "An immediate obedience is the safest and easiest course."[19] There are five "voices" that should harmonize: scripture, conscience, inward impressions, wise counsel and providential circumstances.[20] Tread softly in this arena—guidance is an art, not a science.[3]

First Voice: Scripture

In His Word, God provides boundaries and guidelines so that we can know right and wrong with clarity on many issues and see the general outline of a right path for our lives.[21] We, therefore, need to take the scriptures to heart so that the Holy Spirit may use them to direct us and keep us from error, just as we would study a map to navigate our way through dangerous and unfamiliar terrain.[22] This guidance takes precedence over all else. Hence there is a real need to search the scriptures and keep things in balance. Some general guidelines to follow are "whatever is plainly taught must be obeyed"; "adhere to principles, not isolated texts"; and "keep the main thing, the main thing." The "main thing" is keeping love for Jesus and submission to Him as our first and foremost consideration![23] At times the Lord will even "quicken" His written Word, making it come alive with guidance about specific steps to take. Remember, though, that in Biblical times they didn't have airport searchlights! The lamp that lit their path on a dark night barely showed more than a few steps ahead at a time. He says His Word is like that kind of lamp.[24]

> Rule of Thumb: Don't expect to "hear" a word spoken if it has already been written.
>
> Negative Guidance: The Lord will never lead us contrary to His written Word.
>
> Positive Guidance: General principles of scripture point the way and show the boundaries—but not all is made plain.

Consider this progression: *Good* is the wide range of what He permits by His Word; *better* is trying to find the path of His specific will for you; *best* is actually walking in the center of it!

Second Voice: Conscience

Though not infallible, "Do the next right thing" is a handy way of expressing that aspect of the Spirit-led walk which is a steady succession of "right" ideas to follow supplied by the Spirit to our minds. We are meant to cultivate wisdom and right understanding as one means of being guided by the Lord.[25] We have been given the ability to make right judgments and are expected to use it: "Common sense" is a gift of God; its counterfeit is the natural mind. We have a duty to educate our consciences, renewing our minds by His Word.[26] At the same time we are told not to lean on our understanding at those times when we should be trusting.[27] How do you know it is time to trust? Whenever something happens that you don't understand! Curiously, it is not as hard to "get" wisdom as one might suppose. It's free for the asking, but the catch is you have to have a) the humility to realize you don't have wisdom and b) some basic confidence in His ability to send it your way.[28] There are three "divine guides" that common sense and a reasonably renewed understanding can judge fairly easily:

> Right Desire: Heart and feelings can safely be allowed to lead us if no moral law contradicts the direction they would take.

> Obvious Necessity: Intellect and observation leave no room for doubt about the quick action that is needed in the moment.

> Genuine Duty: The moral call is clear, even if it is undesired, and there is a sense that it would be dishonorable not to do it.

Third Voice: Inward Impressions

Movements of the Holy Spirit upon us, especially when we are "at rest" in the Lord, show us how to move in step with the Spirit.[29] Only the Lord can teach you this way of "continual guidance."[30] Because leadings are often so faint, it really is a process of trial and error. But take heart, He loves it that we are seeking to be led and, after all, He *is* the best Teacher on earth! For instance He instructs us to "walk humbly with our God."[31] Humility is not just the *only* appropriate posture, it actually positions us to receive the wisdom necessary for guidance.[32] Don't be too eager to proclaim that you've heard from the Lord, even if you have. Let events unfold by themselves. His wisdom will become evident to all.[33]

He speaks ever quieter, so we have to learn to become still, if we don't want to miss anything. Quieting our own interior landscape may seem daunting, but it truly is something that we can do.[34] Picture a pond surrounded by trees with the wind blowing and rain pelting the surface. A pebble tossed into it wouldn't be heard or noticed. Then see the pond on a totally calm day: The splash can be heard and every ripple followed to the shore. Now you be that pond and listen for His "pebbles"!

As with our own speech, both the Lord and the enemy have a message (thoughts or words) and an impression (tone of voice). Learn to recognize the ripple effect of their voice upon your soul. The enemy's voice often makes "a splash" that disrupts your inward sense of peace and well-being. The Lord's ripple effect is peace-filled. Listen in quietness for the "still, small voice" and you will catch His gentle whispers.[35] Wait patiently upon Him. It is better to wait for the light to come than to proceed in the dark, but the moment you are sure, yield a complete obedience.

> Rule of Thumb: When in doubt, wait it out; if you feel led, go ahead. Negative impressions (checking, grieving, restraining) caution us to stop, look and listen. Positive impressions (prompting, leading, impelling, calling) lead us forth.

> Warning: Inward impressions may come from wrong spirits or from un-renewed areas of our souls (unhealed wounds, wrong desires, unmet needs, etc.). Proceed with caution! The heart of the old nature is very deceptive.[36] Hannah Whitall Smith cautions, "It is not enough… for the leading to be very 'remarkable,' or the coincidences to be very striking, to stamp it as being surely from God."[37]

Fourth Voice: Consensus of Wise Counsel

The counsel of others is not meant to be a substitute for one's own judgment, since every choice we face is an opportunity for the Lord to grow us in the proper use of the free will He has given us. God will use others to confirm, but rarely to give direction. Agreement of counselors *may* be a sign of God's leading. It needs to be heeded, but not followed slavishly.[38] Who are the wise ones whose walk with the Lord you admire and who God has placed in your life? Make sure you seek them out—not people who will molly-coddle you.[39] Even so, keep in mind that His ultimate purpose is for us to be able to listen for ourselves. It is good to go to others for counsel, but we are not to lean on them—we are to learn to lean only on the Lord.[40]

Fifth Voice: Providential Circumstances

Reading providential signs is for confirmation only. Even open and closed doors are not a sign in themselves: Closed doors need to be respected, but they are not always of the Lord; neither are open doors. As a rule don't force your way past a closed door or turn from it in despair. Learn to wait upon the Lord to open what needs to be opened.[41] However, don't race through every open door you see—it could be a snare. We are meant to let the Shepherd (not signs) go before us, leading us in the way. He *is* the way: Sticking close to Him is the secret of guidance.[42] We are also meant to mature to the point where we can hear and discern His voice. By Jesus' own description "lambs" may not hear His voice, but His "sheep"—those who have matured—certainly do.[43]

> Slow Down Signs: Listen carefully at closed doors; pay attention to hindrances and disturbances "in the flow" of peace.
>
> Proceed With Caution Signs: Open doors and coincidences usually indicate a right path; best of all is the river of joy and peace.

Guidance is different than obedience. With obedience it is "trust Him and *do it*" (the command is clear); with guidance it is "trust Him and *try it*" (a "hunch" is tentative). Trying to be guided is like trying to be good. If you try too hard, you will foul it up by not trusting. Just as His goodness is already there for you to abide in, so is His guidance. Being overly self-conscious is disastrous in anything especially when graceful execution is required. Trust, trust, trust and row your spiritual boat gently down the stream.

Willingness is the coin of the realm where guidance is concerned. Have you ever seen someone trying to get a resistant dog on a leash to walk obediently in the direction and at the pace they desire? Some dogs are rebellious and dig their paws in; some are easily distracted by cats or other dogs. Such dogs may not be taken out beyond necessity and then only under great restraint! Then there are other dogs who don't even need a leash, who go everywhere with their masters. That is our goal—to become so captivated by Jesus in our hearts that we no longer need the sometimes unpleasant discipline of being constrained by Him through our circumstances![44]

Sweet Surrender

If you would love to be readily and frequently guided, then the issue of living with a surrendered heart and a willing spirit is paramount.[45] When Isaiah *saw* the Lord, he fully surrendered and became willing for anything.[46] So would we all! So let's be alert to our innermost thoughts: Even a twinge of unwillingness to surrender is a step towards the Great Rebellion. If you see it in you, you have met the enemy. Carry that thought captive to Christ. Then keep checking to make sure your surrender and willingness stay intact. Let the acronym S.A.A.W. remind you to look to Him.

Father, according to Your love and wisdom,

S. Send: *Send whatever You desire to send*
   (He is the Giver of blessings, never the curse)

A. Allow: *Allow whatever You have to allow*
   (Of free will and its consequences)

A. Ask: *Ask of me whatever You desire or require*
   (Of inward and outward obedience)

W. Withhold: *Withhold me from and Withhold from me*
   (Whatever is necessary to fulfill Your plans)

Make me willing to be made willing to surrender everything to You.

The River of Peace is worth all the battles. There is a vision in Ezekiel of water flowing from the Temple that begins as a shallow stream and eventually becomes a river which no one can cross.[47] This gives us a picture of our life of faith flowing from the place of consecration and surrender, signified by the Temple and its Altar — the place where lives are offered in devotion to the Lord. There is peace as we trust and obey, but at first it is all too easy to step out of the flow of His Spirit's gentle guidance. With practice we can learn to live in the peace Jesus supplies — a peace for our hearts (as we trust Him) and a peace for our feet (as we follow Him). The Holy Spirit is a river of life to all who learn to live in Him and walk by Him. With practice, determined effort, childlike faith and tons of grace this flow of peace and divine purpose, which once was so hard to find (only ankle deep), will become a mighty river that lifts and carries you into great adventures in the Lord. *So what are you waiting for? Go ahead—jump in with both feet!*

For thus says the Lord: "Behold, I will extend peace to her like a river. Isaiah 66:12

Father, forgive me wherever I have thought or said that I have not heard Your voice or experienced Your guidance. I utterly renounce that false belief. The truth is that I am someone who knows how to be guided by You and who has been given ears to hear and eyes to see what You are speaking to me or showing me. I am learning how to listen for Your voice of wisdom through Your Word, through my inner life, and through other people. I am learning to recognize Your Hand—prompting, checking and guiding me. Thank You that You have been speaking to me and guiding me all of my life. Help me to recognize and acknowledge You in all of these ways, so that my eyes can open wider to give You credit and to more readily perceive Your ways of leading me.

Father, according to Your love and wisdom, send whatever You desire to send of Your grace and blessings, allow whatever You have to allow of free will and its consequences, ask of me whatever You desire or require of inward and outward obedience, withhold me from and withhold from me whatever is necessary to fulfill Your plans. Help me to fully trust that You are working in and through all things for my good and Your glory. Make me willing to be made willing to surrender everything to You that I may spend the better part of my days flowing in Your river of peace! May it carry me often into Your Presence and always into Your purposes.

THE WAY OF THE CROSS

And those who belong to Christ Jesus
have crucified the flesh
with its passions and desires.
Galatians 5:24

NEGATIVE EMOTIONS

By now you may be seeing that the negative emotions we live with on a daily basis are actually things that the Lord wants to help us live without. We cannot keep them from ever showing up, but we can certainly learn how to show them the door! Even though we were all issued hearts at birth, few of us were instructed in how to "guard them" with diligence.[1] So let's explore the realm of emotions. Your emotional state holds the key to:

Your enjoyment of daily life   Your relationships with others
Fruitfulness in ministry   Your ability to be guided by God
Success in work   Your ability to enjoy the Lord
Your physical health

Until fairly recently the intelligence quotient (IQ) was seen as the main indicator of a person's likelihood of success in life. Then EQ (emotional intelligence) gained prominence when it was discovered that the leaders of industry usually had moderate IQ, but high EQ—and the high IQ people were all working under them.[2] The good news for us is that unlike intellectual intelligence which rarely changes, emotional intelligence can be increased throughout life with proper cultivation. Emotional intelligence is defined as the ability to understand one's own emotions, empathize with those of others and act appropriately using those emotions, even under stress.[3] From the perspective of these lessons EQ includes the ability to exercise sovereignty over one's own emotional state, carrying every negative emotion that seeks dominance captive to Christ and being restored to confidence, trust and peace—*His emotional life*.

The ABC's of Emotions

Here are some of the ABC building blocks of healthy emotional intelligence. We may not have had them to play with as kids, but we can learn how to use them now.

A. We are sovereigns over our own hearts.
B. We can actually rule over our emotions, rather than be ruled by them—not as a tyrant, but as a listening, learning leader.

C. Left to itself your emotional state will tend to overrule your reason, will and desires—get to it before it gets to you.

D. No one can put an emotion in you and keep it there.

E. You alone get to decide what goes in, stays in and goes out—even though you may not "feel" like you have this ability.

F. All negative emotions are lying to you at *all* times.

G. Even positive emotions will lie to you some times.

H. All emotions spring from what we actually believe to be true.

I. There is a thought/belief at the center of every emotion.

J. Find out what the emotion is telling you and deal with it.

K. Don't blame others for your emotions or you will never get free.

L. Others don't hold the key to what is in you—you do!

M. What you really believe and therefore what you feel is between you and God.

N. God made it that way so that no one can have power over your inner emotional state.

O. No one, not even God, can change your emotions or beliefs without your permission.

P. Your will is free. You are free.

This is truly good news: You are sovereign over your emotions! When it comes to your emotional state you are in charge.[4] It may not feel that way at times, but no one else on the planet can force you to have a feeling or keep it in you if you don't want it. You get to choose what you are going to believe in mind and heart—and *what you deeply believe ultimately determines what you will feel*. Your present emotional reactions are the product of what your heart believes to be true—based on past experiences. These beliefs can be changed! You are actually created with an ability to rule over your emotions, though not by ignoring or over-powering them. The victory is not won by force of will, but by learning to agree deep down with what you know to be true that God is showing you. As new beliefs become rooted in you, your emotions begin to change.

Since ignoring negative emotions doesn't work, be honest about what emotions you are really feeling. Take a good look at them. Don't try to push them down, deny them, or hide them. You are not responsible for what goes off inside of you (so don't bother denying your feelings or feeling guilty for having them), but you are responsible for what you do in response to the feeling that just showed up. Will you let it rule over you or will you carry it captive to Christ so that He and you can begin to rule over that feeling?[5]

In carrying your emotions to Christ, how quickly can an emotional state be shifted? In a heartbeat! How do you shift your emotional state? By getting your eyes back on something about the Lord that releases you and re-empowers you. Just imagine Jesus showing up *right now*. Would seeing His love for you shift your emotional state? Of course it would! Well... *active* faith enables us to see Him and get the shift *whenever* we exercise it.

Failing to master the art of getting our faith focus quickly restored guarantees that a lot of time will be spent in the company of negative emotions. That's not good company! Negative emotions are absolutely no good as spiritual guides. Our negative emotions in and of themselves will never help us to rightly understand other people, our self, God or the world we live in. They are no good at telling us about what is really real or really true from God's perspective—and His perspective is the only one that counts or that will be proven right in the end. Why keep holding on to an emotional life that will never be vindicated as truth? One has to wonder: Do they have *any* redemptive value?

Negative emotions are accurate indicators of our internal (usually hidden) belief system tucked away in the core of our hearts. This is the still unconverted part of us and it needs to hear and be taught to believe the gospel truths that we are beginning to believe (like trusting God, surrendering to God, forgiving others, accepting yourself, etc.). It is not enough to believe these things only in your head. Once your heart begins to believe them, your emotional response to people and situations will shift, but until then there will be a battle on the inside to believe truth. And that is because *negative emotions lie against the truth.*

Negative emotions lie to us and misdirect us. Why would an emotion do that? From the perspective of spiritual warfare, the negative emotion is like a glove; the evil spirit is like an invisible hand manipulating the glove, wanting to squeeze you and mislead you in the process. Think about what you have seen in your own life and that of others in terms of anger with God, fear, hopelessness, self-hatred and unforgiveness as you study these four lies that negative emotions promote.

1) The negative emotion wants to convince you that it has a right to stay as long as the problem exists.

2) It wants to focus you on something or someone else as the problem for why you are stuck with that emotion. It never says: "I'm the problem. Just get rid of me!"

3) It wants to make you think it is up to you to do something about it. It pressures you to be your own savior. It never reminds you to cast that care on the Lord.

4) It wants to get others to agree with it—that it has a right to be in you until the problem "out there" is fixed.

God has created you in such a way that no one and nothing on earth can control your emotional life but you! Whenever negative emotions or emotional pain come on you:

1) It is *always* coming from the enemy's sins against you—so learn to immediately recognize and get indignant at the enemy as the true source of your pain, not other people.[6]

2) If it sticks to you beyond a day it is *always* your sin for holding on to it—so learn to recognize your responsibility and carry that negative emotion to Christ to be set free His way.

3) If you are having a hard time getting free, then the snag is likely coming from deceptive programming the enemy has worked into your innermost beliefs—*seek the Lord* (Chapter 7).

Negative programming comes out of past painful experiences of sins against us combined with our own wrong reactions based on false or ungodly beliefs from the fallen nature. These are the strongholds that we have built up over long periods and they still trap us at times in the mindset of the old nature. Review the lessons on the various strongholds that negative emotions form upon our flesh and pray your heart through the ways in God that these false systems of belief and feeling can be brought down. Where our emotional life is concerned, we really can be the head and not the tail.[7] Let's go for mastery over these pesky invaders of our inner life with Christ!

THE DISCIPLE'S CROSS

Confronted with so much interior disarray, one could easily complain, "This is a lot of work!" True, it's hard dealing with strongholds, but it is harder still letting them rule over us unopposed. No one wants this battle. It is a genuine cross to bear, but because it is a cross, it is also the power of salvation. And that is because there are two crosses that save us. Was that *two* crosses?

Two Crosses that Save Us

Jesus Himself tells us in five separate passages of scripture about the second cross that brings His much needed salvation into our lives.[1] The cross of Jesus saves us by getting us to heaven and by "translating" us into the Kingdom of God on earth.[2] The disciple's cross "saves us" by getting us past the hidden barriers that block us from fully entering into His Kingdom's way of living. It is a major key! We need to understand the disciple's cross and why the Lord allows it—because forsaking the way of the cross will cause us to lose the very life we are trying to save. *How did we miss this?*

> **Then Jesus told his disciples, "If anyone would come after me, let him (1) deny himself and (2) take up his cross and (3) follow me. For whoever would save his life will lose it, but whoever loses his life for my sake will find it."** Matthew 16:24-25

We often stumble at accepting the cross, avoiding being "like our Teacher."[3] Notice the three steps outlined by Jesus which He says are necessary for all who would be His close followers

1) "Deny himself": We are to trust and submit to Jesus letting Him be Lord—not Self. Self wants comfort and immediate gratification, no challenges, struggles or risks. Self wants to be in charge and be at the center. Self is our nemesis, the false god enthroned within us since the Fall. It is hard to give up living for Self if we have a poor image of Father God.

2) "Take up his cross": Derek Prince described the cross as that place "where your will and God's will cross."[4] The cross is never

a person, but it may be a way about them that you don't like and can't easily live with. We "take up" the cross by fully accepting it and the pain that comes with it.

3) "Follow Me": If we are not willing to do steps (1) and (2), how will we ever be able to do step (3)? How will we ever become close followers of Jesus without learning to embrace this cross?

The cross is by no means easy to embrace: It includes learning to endure grief, shame and rejection; it hovers between self-sacrifice and self-denial. Through the cross we learn to say no to Self (*deny yourself*) and yes to God (*take up your cross*) in order to keep walking with our God (*follow Me*). The cross looks like it is bringing death, but it really leads to life. The stakes are high, the onset is painful and the warfare is intense. No wonder the cross can be difficult to discern and hard to accept!

Two Death Dealing Agents

Did you know, for instance, that both the devil and the cross are trying to kill you? There is death by the enemy and death by the cross: The devil wants to kill all that is good and of God in us; the Lord wants to bring to death all that is wrong, all that is not of Christ in us. Furthermore, we are to *resist* the devil, yet we are to *submit* to the Lord.[5] How do you know which is which? How do you know when to submit and when to resist? Here is the key: *We resist the devil in order to embrace the cross.* The enemy always wants us to resist the cross instead!

The cross identifies our places of unrecognized distrust and rebellion, coming out of self-love and self-will. By "blocking" the natural path of our desires, the disciple's cross raises up our "flesh" so that we can deal with it if we want to. The enemy will try to get us to go the wrong way, acting out of our fallen nature. Usually, the hidden side of our self-life just seems like common sense thinking in us, but the cross identifies it as *not of God* or *anti-God*. The Spirit shows us that *in this situation* we will have to deny Self in order to keep following Jesus. A struggle of wills ensues. Under the cross our spirit man still wants to fight Satan, even if we don't.

Likewise, our flesh will often want to fight the Lord, even if we wish we could submit. Perhaps you can relate to the following excerpt from my own diary:

> *The cross reveals my pride, self-will, self-love, self-righteousness and self-protectiveness. So, I hate it. It is not much of a cross if I readily embrace it, not much of a cross if I don't truly want to spurn it at first — and all the more so because of what it makes me see in me.*

We may hate and fear the cross when it first "crosses" our path. We may hate and fear the struggle, pain, loss and risk that comes with it. It helps to know these two ways that God is using the cross:

1) He uses the cross to bring something good into our life we could not have received in any other way. If we could have recognized and crucified that part of our fallen nature on our own, we would have. The passage "through the cross" produces a death to Self in order for us to receive a resurrection into a new quality of life. All we are required to do is "hang in there."

2) In His hands the cross also brings to death that side of us which hates and fears the cross because this too is a part of the self-life in us that doesn't trust the Father's love and wisdom. It needs to be exposed and brought to death for us to live free of those fears. We say "it's killing me," but the truth is that whatever it is in us that is resisting the cross *needs to die.*

Because the cross can be difficult to discern, here are a few ways to help you recognize the cross when it is working on you:

- You can't get rid of it faithfully. You see no way to avoid it either legally in the law or honorably in the Lord.
- It seems to be killing you. You will actually hear yourself saying things like, "This is killing me!" or "I'll just die if…"
- You have to say, "Not my will, but Yours be done" in order to find any peace and freedom.
- There is often a restless search for a way out or around the problem, rather than an acceptance of what cannot be gracefully removed. "In the absence of something better" we have to accept what is presented to us.

- In the way of things, the cross will either be accepted (now) or repeated down the road (in a later trial).

There is great danger in refusing the cross. Jesus warns us that whoever tries to save His life by spurning the cross will lose it.[6] If we seek Self and Self's desires we will lose His kind of life. If we try to rescue our life we will lose it. If we try to protect our life from pain or from the call of God or from loving others or from risk and challenge, we will lose it. If we try to take control of our life (rather than trust God with it), we will lose it. Why are you here? What is your purpose in being here? To cater to Self? Or have you come to do God's will, as Jesus did?[7] True submission to the disciple's cross has been shown to us by the Lord in the way He accepted His own cross. The following is a prayer before the cross modeled on His.

Father, if it is Your will take this cup (the disciple's cross) from me. Nevertheless, not my will but Yours be done. I want to surrender to You in complete confidence and trust, willing to obey and follow Jesus in whatever He asks of me. Make me willing to be made willing.

We need both inner healing and the disciple's cross. Inner healing is often necessary, but it cannot take the place of the disciple's cross, nor remove the pain of it. No amount of inner healing will keep us from encountering the disciple's cross in small or large ways or remove our need for such crosses. However, the healing that comes to us helps restore our trust in the love of the Father, and that does make it easier to see the cross as life-giving, so that we can embrace it more readily. Even the things that we need healing of are themselves forms of the disciple's cross, which we learn to bear gracefully as we seek His healing.

Little crosses prepare us for larger ones. Every minor "crossing" of our will throughout the day prepares us for the larger crosses of life and keeps us in training at surrendering everything to Him. With wisdom we learn to accept our crosses for the same reason Jesus embraced and endured His—for the joy set before us!

Let us run with endurance the race that is set before us, looking to Jesus, the founder and perfecter of our faith, who for the joy that was set before him endured the cross, despising the shame, and is seated at the right hand of the throne of God. Hebrews 12:1-2

ENDNOTES

Preface

[1] John 14:27

Acknowledgements

[1] John 17:17

Chapter 1: The Spiritual Roots of Disease

[1] Colossians 3:3; Romans 8:21
[2] C.S. Lewis, *The Problem of Pain* (New York: MacMillan Publishing Co, Inc. 1962), 93.
[3] Berk, L.S. as quoted by Art Mathias, *In His Own Image* (Anchorage, AK: Wellspring Publishing, 2003), 29.
[4] James 1:17
[5] Don Colbert, MD, *Deadly Emotions* (Nashville, TN: Thomas Nelson Pub., 2003), p. 6.
[6] Ibid., cover.
[7] Ibid., p. 9, 20.
[8] Alexander Loyd, PhD, ND with Ben Johnson, MD, DO, NMD, *The Healing Code* (New York: Grand Central Publishing, 2011), p. 44.
[9] Ibid., p. 97.
[10] Ibid., p. 20-25.
[11] Romans 1:17
[12] Psalm 55:22; Matthew 11:28-30; 1 Peter 5:7
[13] Colossians 3:15
[14] Art Mathias, PhD, *In His Own Image* (Anchorage, AK: Wellspring Ministries of Alaska, 2003), p. 43.
[15] Matthew 22:37-39

Chapter 2: Truth or Consequences

[1] Proverbs 23:7; Matthew 12:34
[2] John 8:44
[3] Hosea 4:6; Isaiah 5:13
[4] Psalm 19:1; Exodus 40:35; 2 Chronicles 5:14
[5] Romans 6:4
[6] Luke 15:11-32; Hebrews 4:16
[7] Genesis 18:25
[8] Romans 8:34; 1 John 4:18; 2 Corinthians 5:19
[9] Exodus 34:7
[10] Exodus 33:7

[11] Deuteronomy 27:1-10
[12] See Deuteronomy 27-28; Proverbs 26:2 KJV
[13] Psalm 103:10
[14] Exodus 34:7
[15] Galatians 6:7-8; Romans 8:28
[16] Matthew 22:36-40
[17] Deuteronomy 28
[18] Isaiah 54:9-10; Romans 8:37-39

Chapter 3: The Keys to the Kingdom

[1] Colossians 1:13
[2] See Romans 3-8 and Galatians for more on justification and righteousness by faith.
[3] Colossians 1:13
[4] Mark 1:15; Luke 17:21
[5] John 3:16
[6] John 3:16; Romans 10:9
[7] Matthew 19:14
[8] Matthew 19:14; Mark 10:14; Luke 18:16
[9] Matthew 16:24-27; Mark 8:34-37; Luke 9:23-25
[10] Mark 11:25
[11] Romans 15:13
[12] John 8:32
[13] John 6:28-29
[14] Luke 11:52; Hebrews 5:14
[15] Psalm 84:5

Chapter 4: Kingdoms in Conflict

[1] Preface, THE SCREWTAPE LETTERS by CS Lewis © copyright CS Lewis Pte Ltd 1942, 1943, 1944, 1952.
[2] Ephesians 6:12
[3] Romans 10:2
[4] Genesis 3:11
[5] See also Mark 9:23-29; Luke 4:40-41; Luke 8:1-2; Luke 13:11-12
[6] 1 Corinthians 6:20; Ephesians 1:14
[7] John 1:5
[8] "We have to learn to fall out of agreement with the compelling force of the spirit's own belief system and believe instead what God's Word declares to be true in situations that trouble us." From Pastor Ed Kelly, Be In Health® teaching and materials, Dr. Henry W. Wright, Thomaston, Georgia, seminar notes, October 2000.
[9] Psalm 35:7
[10] Matthew 22:37
[11] Luke 22:42
[12] Ephesians 6:12
[13] Numbers 14:9

[14] Proverbs 4:23

[15] Henri Nouwen, *The Way of the Heart* (New York: Seabury Press, 1981), pp. 77, 70, 70.

[16] Macarius the Great, cited in Irenee Hausherr, *The Name of Jesus*, trans. Charles Cummings (Kalamazoo, MI: Cistercian Publications, Inc. 1978, p. 314.

[17] Benedicta Ward, trans., *The Sayings of the Desert Fathers* (London & Oxford: Mowbrays, 1975), p. 71.

[18] Ibid. p. 71.

[19] 2 Corinthians 6:7

Chapter 5: Separation from Sin

[1] Exodus 34:7; 2 Corinthians 5:18-19

[2] For the concept of "separation" in relation to justification: Teaching and insights from Be In Health® teaching and materials, Dr. Henry W. Wright, Thomaston, Georgia, seminar notes, October 2000.

[3] Romans 3:24

[4] Isaiah 49:15

[5] 2 Thessalonians 2:13; 1 Peter 2:9

[6] Genesis 1:31

[7] Genesis 3:10

[8] Matthew 16:22-23

[9] 2 Corinthians 5:18-21

[10] Romans 7:22-25

[11] John 8:44-46

[12] 2 Timothy 2:26

[13] Ephesians 6:12

[14] Colossians 1:27

Chapter 6: The Pathway of Temptation

[1] See also Revelation 12:9 for a picture of how vast this work of temptation has become.

[2] Teaching and insights about these seven stages of temptation from Be In Health® teaching and materials, Dr. Henry W. Wright, Thomaston, Georgia, seminar notes, October 2000.

[3] Hebrews 4:16

4 Martin Luther, Letter #1575: to Hieronymous Weller (at Wittenberg), June 19, 1530.

[5] 1 John 3:20

[6] John 15:1-10

[7] John 14:30

[8] Luke 6:45

[9] 2 Timothy 2:24-26

[10] John 8:34

[11] 2 Thessalonians 2:13

[12] Hebrews 5:14

[13] James 1:13

[14] Hebrews 4:16

Chapter 7: Recognize and Replace!

[1] Colossians 3:15
[2] 1 Peter 5:8
[3] Romans 10:13
[4] Hebrews 4:16
[5] For the "R" repetitions in these steps of repentance: Dr. Henry W. Wright, Be In Health®, Thomaston, GA, seminar notes, October 2000.
[6] 2 Timothy 2:25-26
[7] Psalm 51:3-4
[8] Proverbs 23:7; Matthew 15:19; Mark 7:21
[9] James 4:7
[10] Luke 15; Acts 3:19; Hebrews 4:16
[11] Psalm 97:10
[12] 2 Corinthians 10:4-5
[13] Luke 11:20-26
[14] Acts 19:19
[15] James 4:7-8
[16] Ephesians 6:13; Hebrews 12:1-2
[17] John 8:32

Chapter 8: Beholding the True Image

[1] Genesis 3:10
[2] Matthew 6:22-23; 2 Corinthians 4:3-6; 2 Corinthians 5:7; Ephesians 1:18
[3] Deuteronomy 4:15-18
[4] Exodus 20:4-5
[5] Matthew 6:24
[6] "Cascade effect" concept is from a Lance Wallnau teaching, www.LanceLearning.com, message on CD.
[7] Isaiah 51:1; Micah 7:7
[8] Mike Bickle, "Transformation by Beholding Jesus" International House of Prayer Ministry, Kansas City, MO, cassette teachings.
[9] Galatians 2:20
[10] Romans 8:1-4
[11] John 6:63
[12] Ephesians 2:9
[13] Hebrews 7:25

Chapter 9: Our New Identity

[1] John 15:5; Romans 7:18
[2] Philippians 3:7-8

[3] John 3:3-7; 1 Peter 1:23; John 3:16; John 17:3; 1 John 5:11-13
[4] see Romans 7:17-20; 8:1-8; 1 Corinthians 5:5; 2 Colossians 7:1; Galatians 5:13-17, 24-26
[5] Romans 3:24; also see the whole of Romans 3-8 and Galatians
[6] 2 Thessalonians 2:13
[7] Ephesians 2:19; 1 Corinthians 12:27
[8] 2 Corinthians 5:16
[9] Ezekiel 36:26
[10] Jeremiah 31:31-34; 2 Corinthians 5:18-19
[11] Romans 6:5-11
[12] 1 John 1:7; Romans 6:6; Galatians 2:20
[1] Colossians1:27
[2] 1 John 3:2-3
[3] François Fénelon, *Spiritual Letters to Women* (New Canaan, CT: Keats Publishing, Inc., 1980). p. 55.

Chapter 10: The Father's Heart of Love

[1] John 14:9-11
[2] Proverbs 4:23
[3] 1 Corinthians 11:3
[4] "Father Wound" concept and statistics from Gordon Dalbey, *Father and Son* (Nashville, TN: Thomas Nelson, 1992), pp. 4-7.
[5] Romans 3:23
[6] Matthew 3:17; Luke 9:35; John 12:28
[7] Luke 12:32
[8] 1 John 1:5
[9] James 1:17
[10] Proverbs 3:12
[11] Romans 2:4
[12] Matthew 5:44-45
[13] Ephesians 1:5-6
[14] 2 Corinthians 5:19
[15] Romans 3:24
[16] Isaiah 54:7-11
[17] Romans 15:13
[18] John 6:29

Chapter 11: Strongholds

[1] "Strongholds" as emotional and spiritual blocks: Dr. Henry W. Wright, Be In Health®, Thomaston, GA, seminar notes, October 2000.
[2] Ezekiel 36:26
[3] 2 Thessalonians 2:13
[4] Hebrews 12:15

[5] For strongholds as "habit structures of thought": Jack Frost, Shiloh Place Ministry, Myrtle Beach, SC, cassette series. The phrase, "stinking thinking" is attributed to Zig Ziglar.
[6] Jeremiah 17:9
[7] Ezekiel 36:26
[8] Proverbs 4:23
[9] Isaiah 55:8-9
[10] Proverbs 4:5-7; Proverbs 3:5
[11] James 4:7-8
[12] 2 Corinthians 10:4-5
[13] 2 Timothy 2:24-26
[14] Isaiah 5:13; Hosea 4:6
[15] Matthew 15:18-19; Mark 7:21; Hebrews 12:15
[16] Isaiah 30:15

Chapter 12: Reversing the Curse

[1] Genesis 4:10
[2] Lamentations 3:31-33
[3] Daniel 9:1-19
[4] Genesis 1:24
[5] Exodus 34:7
[6] Genesis 1:31
[7] Lamentations 3:52
[8] Robert B. Ewen, An Introduction to Theories of Personality, Third Ed. (Hillsdale, NJ: Lawrence Erlbaum Assoc., Publishers, 1988) p. 523.
[9] Thomas Verny, MD, The Secret Life of the Unborn Child (New York, NY: Dell Publishing, 1981) p. 49.
[10] Teaching and insights about these three ways that generational curses are transmitted from Be In Health® teaching and materials, Dr. Henry W. Wright, Thomaston, Georgia, seminar notes, October 2000.
[11] see Leviticus 19:31 for "familiar spirits"
[12] Compiled. The survey on the Jukes family was done by Richard Dugdale in 1877; the one on Edward's family was done by A. E. Winship in 1900. There are exaggerated versions on the web, but these figures go back to the original reports.
[13] 1 Thessalonians 2:11; 1 Timothy 5:1

Chapter 13: The Power of Believing

[1] Ephesians 2:8
[2] James 2:19
[3] Ephesians 2:8
[4] Romans 15:13
[5] Romans 15:13
[6] Hebrews 4:1-2
[7] Acts 16:25

[8] Mark 6:5-6
[9] Psalms 56:4 and 119:81
[10] Philippians 4:7
[11] John 15:1-17
[12] Hebrews 4:11
[13] James 1:16
[14] Genesis 1:1-3
[15] John 17:17
[16] Numbers 23:19
[17] John 4:23
[18] Genesis 15:1-6
[19] Romans 4:16-25
[20] Proverbs 3:5; Romans 8:14
[21] Romans 8:37-39
[22] Mark 9:23-24

Chapter 14: Discerning the Enemy

[1] 2 Corinthians 2:10-11
[2] Hebrews 5:14
[3] Mark 11:25
[4] 1 Samuel 24:6
[5] James 1:14
[6] Genesis 3:1-5; Job 1:9
[7] 1 Corinthians 4:3-4
[8] Genesis 3:11-13; Job 2:4; Zechariah 3:3; Luke 9:56
[9] Romans 8:32-35
[10] Galatians 6:1-2
[11] Revelation 12:7-11
[12] Genesis 3:1-5
[13] John 8:31-38
[14] Genesis 3:11
[15] Teaching and insights stemming from "Who told you?"and accusation as a block to healing from Be In Health® teaching and materials, Dr. Henry W. Wright, Thomaston, Georgia, seminar notes, October 2000.
[16] Genesis 3:9-13
[17] Hebrews 5:14; Matthew 7:1-5
[18] 2 Corinthians 10:3-6
[19] Hebrews 7:25
[20] Matthew 5:7, 7:2; Luke 6:38

Chapter 15: Freedom through Forgiving

[1] Luke 6:37-38
[2] 2 Corinthians 10:3-6

³ Art Matthias PhD., Wellsprings Ministries of Alaska, Anchorage, Alaska, seminar notes, Hilton Head, SC. January 2006.
⁴ Teaching and insights concerning this sevenfold progression of bitterness and bitterness as a block to healing from Be In Health® teaching and materials, Dr. Henry W. Wright, Thomaston, Georgia, seminar notes, October 2000.
⁵ John 14:15
⁶ Matthew 18:34-35
⁷ Luke 23:34
⁸ Matthew 18:33
⁹ 2 Timothy 2:24-26
¹⁰ Psalm 84:5
¹¹ Exodus 22:7
¹² Job 42:10

Chapter 16: Mending the Broken Heart

¹ For this excellent definition of a broken heart: Art Mathias PhD., seminar notes, op. cit.
² Matthew 10:24
³ 2 Corinthians 4:17
⁴ Random House, *Webster's College Dictionary* (New York: McGraw-Hill, 1991).
⁵ A.A. *Alcoholics Anonymous* (New York: Alcoholics Anonymous World Services, Inc. 2001), p. 59. Quotation frequently cited in reference to Step 4: "Made a searching and fearless moral inventory of ourselves."
⁶ Luke 4:18-19
⁷ Matthew12:34-35
⁸ Proverbs 23:7
⁹ Matthew 11:12
¹⁰ Matthew 5:4
¹¹ 1 Thessalonians 4:13
¹² James 5:16
¹³ Mark 11:25-27
¹⁴ Zechariah 9:12; Joel 2:25

Chapter 17: Accepted in the Beloved

¹ Hebrews 13:15
² John 8:32
³ 1 Peter 5:8; Genesis 3:1: a lion seeking to devour and a serpent bringing accusations.
⁴ Teaching and insights about these five components of rejection from Be In Health® teaching and materials, Dr. Henry W. Wright, Thomaston, Georgia, seminar notes, October 2000.
⁵ Mark 12:30
⁶ Romans 16:25: the gospel of grace is what "grounds" us, establishing our hearts.
⁷ 2 Corinthians 5:19
⁸ 2 Corinthians 5:7

[9] Teaching and insights about these four coping strategies from Be In Health® teaching and materials, Dr. Henry W. Wright, Thomaston, Georgia, seminar notes, October 2000.

[10] Colossians 3:3

[11] Psalm 139:14-15

[12] Isaiah 53:3

[13] 2 Corinthians 5:21

[14] Hebrews 4:15

[15] Matthew 27:46

[16] Hebrews 13:5

[17] 2 Corinthians 1:20

Chapter 18: Love Thyself!

[1] *Love is patient and kind; love does not envy or boast; it is not arrogant or rude. It does not insist on its own way; it is not irritable or resentful; it does not rejoice at wrongdoing, but rejoices with the truth. Love bears all things, believes all things, hopes all things, endures all things. Love never ends.* 1 Corinthians 13:4-8

[2] Romans 8:1

[3] Revelation 3:10

[4] 2 Corinthians 12:9-10

[5] Galatians 3:24

[6] James 1:5

[7] Acts 17:26

[8] Isaiah 40:31

[9] 1 Peter 3:3

[10] Genesis 3:11

[11] Romans 3:4

[12] Psalm 139:14

[13] John 15:5

14 Art Mathias, PhD, *In His Own Image* (Anchorage, AK: Wellspring Ministries of Alaska, 2003), pp. 25, 44.

[15] Teaching and insights about self-pity as the "super-glue from hell that binds us to our past" and the relationship of self-rejection to the auto-immune disorders from Be In Health® teaching and materials, Dr. Henry W. Wright, Thomaston, Georgia, seminar notes, October 2000.

[16] Psalm 18:34

[17] *I am not what I was. I am not what I will be. I am being changed from glory to glory. And God is loving me full throttle all along the way!* From the "Unloving Spirit" cassette series, Be In Health® teaching and materials, Dr. Henry W. Wright, Thomaston, Georgia, 2000.

[18] John 15:11, 16:24

Chapter 19: Godly Contentment

[1] Ephesians 1:11-18; Colossians 1:12; 1 Peter 1:4

[2] G. K. Chesterton, *St. Francis of Assisi* (Garden City, NY: Image Books, 1957), p. 75.

[3] Philippians 4:7; John 14:27

[4] Teaching and insights about the relationship of envy to the immune system and the role of coveting, pride and comparison from Be In Health® teaching and materials, Dr. Henry W. Wright, Thomaston, Georgia, seminar notes, October 2000.

[5] James 3:14-17

[6] James 4:1-4

[7] Matthew 6:33

[8] Ephesians 5:3-5; Colossians 3:5

[9] 1Timothy 6:3-5

[10] James 3:14-16

[11] Acts 10:34-35; Romans 2:11

[12] Matthew 6:33; Psalm 37:3-5; Psalm 73:25

[13] Genesis 15:1

[14] Malachi 3:8-12

[15] 1 Corinthians 3:21-23

[16] Jeremiah 33:11; Hebrews 13:15

[17] St. Augustine of Hippo (354-430 AD), *The Confessions*.

[18] Luke 21:19

[19] see also Psalms 27:14 and 130:6; Micah 7:7

[20] Isaiah 40:31; Isaiah 64:4; Lamentations 3:26

Chapter 20: Exposing the Darkness

[1] Revelation 2:24

[2] Pastor Wade Trimmer, sermon notes, Grace Fellowship of Augusta, GA, March 2006.

[3] Exodus 22:18-20; Leviticus 20:6-8, 27

[4] Exodus 20:3-6; 2 Corinthians 10:4-6

[5] Exodus 20:3; Deuteronomy 5:7: "You shall have no other gods before Me."

[6] Isaiah 47:13; Daniel 2:2; Matthew 24:11: "the astrologers, the stargazers, the monthly prognosticators" are all condemned.

[7] Leviticus 19:31, 20:6; Isaiah 8:19, 19:3: "Give no regard to mediums."

[8] 1 Sammuel 15:23; 2 Kings 17:17, Acts 8:9; Galatians 5:20: "Rebellion is as the sin of witchcraft."

[9] *Webster's College Dictionary*, op. cit.

[10] Teaching and insights about the occult analogy from astronomy from Be In Health® teaching and materials, Dr. Henry W. Wright, Thomaston, Georgia, seminar notes, October 2000.

[11] Proverbs 7:23; 14:12

[12] Mormonism began when Joseph Smith was visited by the angel Moroni who showed him a "different gospel."

[13] 1 Samuel 15:23

[14] Teaching and insights about the occult connection to pharmaceutical abuse from Be In Health® teaching and materials, Dr. Henry W. Wright, Thomaston, Georgia, seminar notes, October 2000.

[15] Deuteronomy 30:11-19

[16] Deuteronomy 30:17-18

[17] Proverbs 10:12 and 17:9

[18] Ephesians 5:11

[19] Romans 14:13-14
[20] Titus 1:15
[21] Proverbs 14:12
[22] Acts 19:18-20

Chapter 21: Fear Not!

[1] 1 John 4:18-19
[2] Matthew 6:25-34; Mark 4:35-40
[3] Hebrews 11:1
[4] Job 3:24-26
[5] Numbers 13:30-33
[6] Romans 14:23
[7] Romans 8:15
[8] 2 Timothy 1:7 KJV and NKJV
[9] Modified from a list by Pastor Ed Kelly: Be In Health® teaching and materials, Dr. Henry W. Wright, Thomaston, Georgia, seminar notes, October 2000.
[10] 1 John 4:18-19
[11] Isaiah 26:3
[12] 1 John 4:9-10
[13] Romans 10:17
[14] James 4:7-8
[15] Proverbs 17:22
[16] Hebrews 12:14-15
[17] Luke 9:23-25
[18] Philippians 4:6-7
[19] Hebrews 5:14
[20] Matthew 14:25
[21] 2 Corinthians 12:9; Hebrews 4:16

Chapter 22: No More Idols!

[1] Genesis 4:6-7
[2] Romans 6:6
[3] John 10:10
[4] Genesis 25:29-34
[5] 1 Corinthians 10:13
[6] John 14:9-11 and 17:1-5
[7] See Ecclesiastes 4:12 for the metaphor of a threefold cord's strength.
[8] Bruce Marshall, *The World, the Flesh and Father Smith* (Boston, MA: Houghton Mifflin Company, 1945), p. 108. Often mistakenly attributed to G. K. Chesterton.
[9] 2 Corinthians 10:4-6
[10] Ephesians 2:8
[11] Romans 10:12-13
[12] 2 Thessalonians 2:10
[13] Romans 6:6; 7:5-6; 8:10-11; Galatians 2:19-21

14 Romans 8:13; 13:12-14; Galatians 5:22-25; Ephesians 4:20-24; Colossians 3:1-5
15 Matthew 11:12; Ephesians 6:13; Exodus 14:13; Zechariah 4:6

Chapter 23: Spiritual Warfare 101

1 Matthew 7:14 WEB
2 Luke 18:16
3 John H. Sammis (1846-1919), lyrics: *Trust and Obey.*
4 Matthew 22:38
5 Galatians 2:20
6 Colossians 3:15
7 Proverbs 4:23
8 Isaiah 64:8; Romans 9:21
9 Matthew 11:27
10 2 Corinthians 4:6
11 1 Peter 5:6
12 Romans 9:22-24
13 Galatians 5:22
14 James 1:14
15 Jack Deere, seminar notes, MorningStar Ministry, Charlotte, NC. September 2005.
16 Nehemiah 4:17-18; Isaiah 60:18
17 1 Timothy 6:12; 2 Timothy 4:7

Chapter 24: Walking in the Spirit

1 Galatians 5:25
2 Psalm 138:2
3 Ephesians 5:25
4 1 Corinthians 6:17; Ephesians 1:13
5 Job 33:4; Genesis 2:7; John 20:22
6 Ephesians 2:8
7 Isaiah 46:3-4
8 Matthew 18:2-4
9 Isaiah 11:6; Mark 10:15; Luke 18:17
10 Isaiah 42:5
11 John 14:16-18
12 John 1:4, 9
13 Saint Augustine of Hippo (354-430), Seventh Homily on 1st John
14 Galatians 2:20
15 Proverbs 3:5-6
16 Hannah Whitall Smith, *The Christian's Secret of a Happy Life* (New York, NY: Ballantine Books, 1986), p. 81.
17 Ephesians 5:17-18
18 1 Kings 22:7-8 especially verse 8.
19 Smith, op. cit., p. 79.

[20] Ibid., p 72. The "voices" of guidance are expanded from the chapter "Difficulties Concerning Guidance." The consensus of wise counsel has been added to the four "voices" listed in *The Christian's Secret* op. cit.

[21] See Psalm 119—all of it.

[22] John 17:17

[23] Mark 12:30: the first commandment is our foremost assignment and abiding purpose.

[24] Psalms 119:105

[25] Proverbs 4:5-7

[26] Romans 12:2; 2 Thessalonians 2:13

[27] Proverbs 3:5-6

[28] James 1:5-6

[29] Hebrews 5:14

[30] Isaiah 58:11

[31] Micah 6:8

[32] James 4-6

[33] Matthew 11:19

[34] Psalm 131:1-3

[35] 1 Kings 19:12

[36] Jeremiah 17:9

[37] Smith, 76

[38] Proverbs 15:22

[39] Proverbs 13:14

[40] Jeremiah 31:34

[41] Revelation 3:7-8

[42] John 14:6

[43] John 10:3-4, 27

[44] Psalm 32:8-9

[45] Psalm 51:10-12: Sustain with a "right" spirit is also translated "willing" spirit.

[46] Isaiah 6:1-8

[47] Ezekiel 47:1-5

Negative Emotions

[1] Proverbs 4:23

[2] Dr. Lance Wallnau during a Kingdom Business Assoc. conference at MorningStar Ministry, Charlotte, NC. January 2009.

[3] Daniel Coleman, *Working with Emotional Intelligence* (London: Bloomsbury Publishing, 1998) p. 7.

[4] Proverbs 4:23

[5] 2 Corinthians 10:4-6

[6] 2 Timothy 2:24-26

[7] Deuteronomy 28:13-14

The Disciple's Cross

[1] Matthew 10:38, 16:24; Mark 8:34; Luke 9:23, 14:27

[2] Colossians 1:13

[3] Matthew 10:24; Luke 6:40

[4] Derek Prince, *The Christian Life Series: The Grace of Yielding* (Ft. Lauderdale, FL: Messages by Derek Prince, 1982), Cassette teaching, message number 19.

[5] *Submit yourselves therefore to God. Resist the devil, and he will flee from you. Draw near to God, and he will draw near to you.* James 4:7-8

[6] Matthew 10:38

[7] Hebrews 10:9

BIBLIOGRAPHY

The Mind Body Connection and Inner Healing

Art Mathias. *In His Own Image.*

Don Colbert, MD. *Deadly Emotions.*

Henry Wright. *A More Excellent Way.*

John and Paula Sanford. *The Transformation of the Inner Man.*

Neil T. Anderson. *The Bondage Breaker.*

The Father's Heart

Gordon Dalbey. *Father and Son: The Wound, The Healing, The Call to Manhood.*

Hannah Whithall Smith. *The God of All Comfort.*

Henri J. M. Nouwen. *The Return of the Prodigal Son.*

Classics of the Spiritual Life

A. W. Tozer. *The Attributes of God; The Knowledge of the Holy; God's Pursuit of Man.*

Andrew Murray. *Humility.*

Brother Lawrence. *The Practice of the Presence of God.*

C. S. Lewis. *Mere Chrisitianity.*

François Fénelon. *Spiritual Letters to Women; Mediations on the Heart of God.*

Hannah Whithall Smith. *The Christian's Secret of a Happy Life.*

Jeanne Guyon. *Experiencing the Depths of Jesus Christ; Intimacy with Christ.*

Roy and Revel Hession. *The Calvary Road.*

Thomas A Kempis. *The Imitation of Christ.*

Watchman Nee. *Sit, Walk, Stand; The Release of the Spirit.*

Spiritual Warfare

Derek Prince. *Blessing or Curse.*

Francis MacNutt. *Deliverance from Evil Spirits.*

Johanna Michaelsen. *The Beautiful Side of Evil.*

Rebecca Brown. *He Came to Set the Captives Free; Prepare for War.*

HEALING STREAMS MINISTRY

Healing Streams is a ministry of liberation and transformation founded by Steve Evans and his first wife, June, the year before she died. It is now being carried on by Steve and Eunice Evans. Through Biblical teaching we seek to help people find freedom from the negative emotions that rob inner peace and damage health. Our main healing lessons form a 24 part series, *Matters of the Heart*, which can be accessed for free through our website as individual, downloadable teachings in PDF and MP3 formats or viewed on our Youtube channel.

Contact us at
info@healingstreamsusa.org
Visit us on the web at
www.healingstreamsusa.org
www.youtube.com/healingstreamsusa
www.facebook.com/healingstreamsusa

Healing Streams Ministry is a division of Forerunner Ministries, Inc., a 501(c)3 nonprofit corporation (Federal Tax ID# 030557651).

THE eCOURSE FOR HEALING

www.healingstreamsusa.org

Practically everyone needs recovery of their heart from some painful issues of the past or could readily benefit from gaining mastery over their emotional turbulence in the present. The peace of Christ is meant to be a river of life that we experience all day long—no matter what our circumstances may be. Let the 24 main healing lessons and workout sessions of our eCourse take your heart on pilgrimage to a place called the Kingdom of God that is already right inside you!

SPIRIT FILLED LIVING

www.forerunners4Him.org

Whether you are a brand new recruit or a "seasoned veteran", if you find that your peace levels are slipping and your joy is not full, then everything on this site is designed to help you come into the fullness of what it truly means to be saved by grace through faith— in all of your days and all of your situations. And it is all available for free!

For us a forerunner is anyone who receives salvation and begins a lifetime quest of "running" into the heart of God for intimacy and going before the Lord in devoted service to prepare His way into other lives. That's your heart too, isn't it? Come get the equipping you need to be a liberated lover of Jesus and a loving liberator of others.

BOOKS FROM FORERUNNER

If you enjoyed *The Missing Peace*, consider purchasing copies for friends at www.createspace.com/37853819 and keep exploring the spiritual life through these other insightful books by Steve Evans, available at Amazon.com and Healingstreamsusa.org. Series, Vol. 3.

Matters of the Heart is a 24 lesson workbook designed to guide Christian believers through the basic understandings necessary for releasing emotional damage from the past and gaining a grace-based restoration to wholeness. Each chapter is filled with "tools" for practical application.
278 pages. Paperback: $20.00.

Rescued from Hell chronicles one man's journey into a ten year living nightmare and his astonishing true story of return. Was it an insane delusion or a satanic deception? This is a tale both incredible and terrible, yet studded with life affirming humor and hope-filled insights into the spiritual realities that surround us.
190 pages. Paperback: $12.50.

An Illustrated Guide to the Spiritual Life captures in living color with playful insights the otherwise elusive, invisible realities of our life in God. This "illustrated devotional" includes explanations, scriptures and prayers. It is written for the general reader, but is also a pictorial companion to *The Missing Peace*.
56 pages. Paperback: $10.00.
The River of Peace Series, Vol. 1.

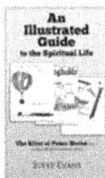

Good Grief is not for everyone, but for those who despite their pain have "set their hearts on pilgrimage", determined to make it to the other side of the Valley of Tears, allowing sorrow that is *rightly* carried to mend their hearts and guide their lives toward God's new beginning.

70 pages. Paperback: $10.00.

The River of Peace Series, Vol. 2.

Salvation Basics provides easy to understand answers to life's most important questions: "What will happen to me when I die?" and "What can I do about it?" You will not only discover God's grace-filled way for getting you to heaven, but also His "secret" for living the heavenly life down here.

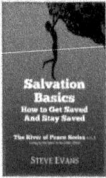

118 pages. Paperback: $10.00.

The River of Peace Series, Vol. 3.

Ministry Basics will prepare you to launch into the sea of human need, lostness and misery which surrounds you, finding your place in the Rescue and your highest path of purpose at the Lord's side. Let these field-tested truths equip you for a joy-filled lifetime of Holy Spirit empowered ministry.

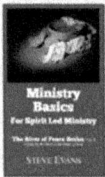

163 pages. Paperback: $10.00.

The River of Peace Series, Vol. 4.

www.ingramcontent.com/pod-product-compliance
Lightning Source LLC
Chambersburg PA
CBHW051828090426
42736CB00011B/1704